Lysistrata

Aristophanes

Lysistrata

Translated,
with Notes and Topical Commentaries, by
Sarah Ruden

Hackett Publishing Company, Inc.
Indianapolis/Cambridge

25 24 23 22 21   5 6 7 8 9

For further information, please address

Hackett Publishing Company, Inc.
P.O. Box 44937
Indianapolis, IN 46244-0937

www.hackettpublishing.com

For information regarding performance rights,
please email us at permissions@hackettpublishing.com

Cover art: *Lysistrata and the Old Men,* by Norman Lindsay.
Copyright © H. A. & C. Glad. Reprinted with permission.

Cover design by Brian Rak and Jean Whitman
Composition by William Hartman

Library of Congress Cataloging-in-Publication Data

Aristophanes.
    [Lysistrata. English]
    Lysistrata / Aristophanes; translated, with notes and topical
    commentaries, by Sarah Ruden.
       p. cm.
    Includes bibliographical references and index.
    ISBN 0-87220-604-1 (cloth) — ISBN 0-87220-603-3 (paper)
    1. Greece—History—Peloponnesian War, 431–404 B.C.—
    Drama. 2. Lysistrata (Fictitious character)—Drama. 3. Peace
    movements—Drama. I. Ruden, Sarah. II. Title.

PA3877 .L8 2003
882'.01—dc21   2002038750

ISBN-13: 978-0-87220-604-5 (cloth)
ISBN-13: 978-0-87220-603-8 (pbk.)

Contents

Preface

I have esteemed Aristophanes' *Lysistrata* since before I read a line
of it. I heard as a teenager that one Greek comedy was about
women placing an embargo on sex until their warring husbands
made peace. "That must be a great story," I said, lifting my head
from Rousseau's *Confessions*, which I had pulled from the family
bookshelf and was searching in vain for dirty scenes.

When I got my hands on a *Lysistrata* translation, however, I
was disappointed. The play was naughty enough, but somehow
heavy and prim, too, and not particularly amusing. Long afterward, in studying ancient Greek, I discovered the pitfalls of translating Greek comedy: the humor in a line might depend on a
particle, an element that does not exist in English but that Greeks
could hardly utter a sentence without; an object or institution
referred to might be AWOL from modern experience and have no
functional equivalent; a joke that might have had Athenians
gasping and scrambling for the latrines may just not be funny to
us, though the gist is conveyed clearly.

Yet translations of comedy that left me stone-faced still
seemed sick and wrong, and I persisted in thinking that more
could be done. Sadly, I did not come across the excitement of
Douglass Parker's work until much later—or not so sadly: it was
better for me to address certain problems on my own than to
imitate his methods, as I would no doubt have done in my hero-
starved youth.

My commentaries on Greek history and culture are like those
on Rome attached to my translation of the *Satyricon* of Petronius,
only somewhat longer. I have written them in the same spirit, one
many readers said they found welcoming and helpful. Neither
here nor there have I made any attempt at comprehensive sur-
veys of scholarship or in-depth historical narration. Those exist
elsewhere, in giddy plenty. These commentaries are an effort to
offer something I regret not having had when my own interest in
classics surfaced: a resource that is both basic and—without apol-
ogies—entertaining. This effort has been a natural accompani-
ment to my ambitions in translating.

Aristophanes, the Other Gadfly of Athens

Aristophanes was born around 450 and probably died in 385 B.C.E. He was therefore a contemporary of, among others, Socrates (469–399 B.C.E.) and Plato (c. 429–347 B.C.E.). Like them, he was a citizen of the city-state of Athens. His family may have owned property on the island of Aegina. Two of his plays were produced by his son Araros, who wrote his own comedies as well.

In Plato's *Symposium*, a literary account of a drinking party that purportedly took place in 416 B.C.E., we come the closest to a reliable view of Aristophanes' personality. At that time, Plato was around thirteen years old. He makes no claim of a better than thirdhand knowledge of the party, but growing up in Athens' relatively small circle of the well-to-do and intensely cultured, he would have known Aristophanes, whom he portrays as a drinker and a womanizer, a genial partygoer, and a lively oral storyteller; the playwright alludes to himself in more or less the same way in certain of his works.

Aristophanes wrote more than forty plays, of which eleven survive, making him, aside from a few fragments of other writers, our only representative of Old Comedy (fifth century B.C.E.), the rollicking political drama that preceded the transitions of Middle Comedy (roughly 404–321 B.C.E.) and the soap operas of New Comedy (after about 321 B.C.E., but without even a vaguely visible finish line).

Clear into the time Aristophanes himself was helping to shape Middle Comedy, his comedies—despite their often fantastical premises—were fairly consistently concerned with contemporary politics and social institutions. His approach tended to be mildly aristocratic but sympathetic to the struggles of the common people; patriotic but against jingoism; suspicious of social innovation; cynical about corruption but without specific and practical plans for reform; unrestrained in insult; and—this is perhaps his most vivid attraction today—exuberantly bawdy. If he were a modern performance artist, he would call members of the audience up onto the stage, give them wedgies, and comment on the shape of their behinds. No, he was worse: one gibe of his is "gaping anus'd," or disfigured from too much anal sex. By his favorite early target, the demagogue Cleon, he was prosecuted twice—with how much success, scholars' opinions vary. The somewhat milder nature of his later but still political plays may be due to more caution, or simply to more maturity.

The Peloponnesian War (431–404 B.C.E.), which began in his youth and ended in his middle age, is his single most frequent topic in the extant plays. *Acharnians* and *Lysistrata* are wholly directed toward lobbying for peace, and *Peace* celebrates a treaty with the Spartans. Other plays as well contain antiwar exhortation. The loss of the war and the consequent changes Athenian public life underwent may have done much to shift Aristophanes' themes out of the realm of public policy.

A Comedy with Legs

Aristophanes' work is uneven. I doubt that even professional classicists would read a mass of mean-spirited vituperation like *Knights* or a going-through-the-motions allegory like *Wealth* unless they had to. Critics disagree whether *Clouds*, *Birds*, *Lysistrata*, or *Frogs* is the greatest play, but the question is literally academic; those who know the Greek language and the social history of Athens most intimately must fight out among themselves where the author achieved the best effects. But I cannot understand any hesitation about which play is most suitable as an introduction to Aristophanes. *Clouds* lampoons the unique contemporary education scene, and parts of it cannot make sense to an audience unversed in Greek grammatical gender. *Birds* perches on a thin, glittery frame of untranslatable avian jokes. *Frogs* burps through a long critique of the tragic poets Euripides and Aeschylus, even comparing meters; you definitely had to be there.

But the women's sexual strike in *Lysistrata* is a tale for all seasons. "Hey, women ought to do that now," said people I talked to about it. And the telling, as well as the tale, is inviting. Specialized language is sparse and cultural barriers low, because the characters spend much of their time talking, yelling, whining, and muttering about a universal physical drive. The complaints about military spending are recognizable, even if it was the more conservative Athenians wanting cutbacks. Fear of foreigners and contempt for self-enriching cliques sound only too familiar. *Lysistrata* offers by far the best odds of *getting* Greek comedy while getting some fun out of it.

In its aesthetics and its humanity also, this play really stands out. It was produced at a low point for Athens in the war (411 B.C.E.) and is full of anxiety for peace. Its chorus is divided evenly

between men and women. These groups fight each other, sym-
bolizing pervasive societal conflict. They effectively take over the
traditional *agon* (debate) from the protagonist and her opponent:
Lysistrata snarls the Councilor down, and he has no real opportunity to state his opposing views, but the semichoruses quarrel for
long periods—mostly with physical threats and personal insults,
however, and mostly without the forward-pushing intellectual
exchange expected in an *agon*. Theirs is some of the least con-
structive disagreement in all of Aristophanes. The *parabasis* (choral speech on behalf of the author) falls away, because the divided
chorus have no chance to give it. Although one set of opinions is
clearly right, the two are more than usually well-balanced against
each other in their power and presence. Yet despite this, the semichoruses finally reconcile through the women's acts of banal
kindness—a suggestion that living in peace is easy and natural,
once people make up their minds to do it.

There is nothing more striking in this play than the character
of Lysistrata. She may seem nobler and less selfish than all but
one or two other Old Comedy protagonists—but she has, thank
goodness, a bracing cynicism and none of the posing virtues of
modern heroines. She is just wonderful to have around, comfort-
ing and inspiriting as well as entertaining, a Joan of Arc you can
go to a bar with.

Acknowledgments

I hate you all. You leave me writhing to give a decent account of
what you have done for me, and no matter what I say, I am still
going to feel like an ungrateful little weasel. Thanks to the
optimi magistri at Bowling Green State University, who started
me in classics, mostly on their own time, out of the pure hope of
passing down the discipline. Thanks to Jeffrey Henderson, who
taught me the bulk of my Greek and introduced me to comedy,
and whose 1987 Oxford edition of the play was the main one I
used. Thanks to David Ross, who first helped me formulate
problems in translation, and to Richard Tarrant, who took the
project further. Thanks to Peter Horn, David Friedland, and
Ben Williams, dear critics and encouragers. Thanks to Brian
Rak, my swell editor. Thanks most of all to Harris; I won't say
why, for fear that readers will toss this book away in irritation
at my sappiness.

Cast of Characters

Speaking Characters

LYSISTRATA
CALONICE
MYRRHINE
LAMPITO
MEN'S CHORUS LEADER
CHORUS OF OLD MEN
WOMEN'S CHORUS LEADER
CHORUS OF OLD WOMEN
COUNCILOR
OLD WOMEN #1, #2, AND #3
WOMEN #1, #2, AND #3
CINESIAS
CINESIAS' BABY
SPARTAN HERALD
UNITED CHORUS
UNITED CHORUS LEADER
SPARTAN AMBASSADOR
ATHENIAN AMBASSADORS #1 AND #2

Nonspeaking Characters

ATHENIAN WOMEN
BOEOTIAN WOMAN
CORINTHIAN WOMAN
SPARTAN AND OTHER FOREIGN WOMEN
FEMALE SCYTHIAN GUARD
TWO SLAVES
FOUR MALE SCYTHIAN GUARDS
CINESIAS' SLAVE
ATHENIAN AMBASSADORS
SPARTAN AMBASSADORS
THE AMBASSADORS' SLAVES
RECONCILIATION
PIPER

Lysistrata

SCENE: *A large rectangular stage behind a bare circular area with an altar in the middle. Two ramplike entrances to the circular area at the left and right. A stage building with up to three doors in front, and a hatch to allow actors onto the roof. Scene descriptions and stage directions occur nowhere in an ancient Greek dramatic text, but the context here suggests that the action begins on the lower slopes of the Acropolis or in an Athenian residential district. The action later moves to the outside of the Propylaea, or ceremonial gates leading to the top of the Acropolis, then probably to lower Athens again, and then to the outside of a banqueting hall. But the action should be considered continuous or nearly continuous: a Greek chorus remained the whole time after its entrance, and scene changes in an open-air theater with no curtain would have been sketchy.*

(Enter Lysistrata, a good-looking young matron.)

LYSISTRATA:[1]
    If I'd invited them to hoot and prance
    At Bacchic rites, or at some sleazy shrine,[2]
    I would have had to crawl through tambourines
    To get here. As it is, no woman's showed,
    Except my neighbor Calonice.[3] Hi.   5

(Enter Calonice, a middle-aged matron.)

CALONICE:
    Hi, Lysistrata. Honey, what's gone wrong?

---

1. The name means "Dissolver of Armies." A real woman, the contemporary priestess of Athena Polias ("of the City"), appears to have had a similar name, Lysimache ("Dissolver of Combat").

2. Women gathered at special shrines to hold certain single-sex religious rites. Aristophanes names four spots: "a place of Bacchic revelry" (for rites of Dionysus, the wine god), "a [grotto] of Pan" (a rural god), "Colias" (site of a sanctuary of Aphrodite, the goddess of erotic love), and "a [shrine] of Genetyllis" (a goddess of childbirth). A suspicion of drunkenness and even of sexual license hovered over the events, nearly the only ones in which men could not control women's behavior.

3. "Beautiful Victory."

Don't spoil your pretty face with ratty snarls!
Your eyebrows look like bows to shoot me dead.

LYSISTRATA:
Oh, Calonice, this just burns me up.
10   Women are slacking off, can't make the grade.
Our husbands say we're cunning to the point
Of—well—depravity.

CALONICE:
                    Darn tootin' right!

LYSISTRATA:
But given word to meet me here today—
A vital matter needs our serious thought—
They're sleeping in.

CALONICE:
15   But sweetie, soon they'll come.
Sometimes it's quite a challenge sneaking out.
The husband might require some straightening up,
The maid a screech to get her out of bed,
The kid a bath, a nibble, or a nap.

LYSISTRATA:
20   But what I have to say means more than that
To women.

CALONICE:
            Precious, what *is* eating you?
Why summon us in this mysterious way?
What is it? Is it . . . big?

LYSISTRATA:
                    Of course.

CALONICE:
                        And hard?

LYSISTRATA:
Count on it.

CALONICE:
            Then how could they not have *come?*

LYSISTRATA:
25   Oh, shut your mouth. They *would* have flocked for that.

No, this thing I've gone through exhaustively;
I've worked it over, chewed it late at night.

CALONICE:
Pathetic if it needed that much help.

LYSISTRATA:
It's this pathetic: in the women's hands
Is the salvation of the whole of Greece.   30

CALONICE:
In women's hands? It's hanging by a thread.

LYSISTRATA:
We hold within our grasp the city's plight.
The Peloponnesians may be wiped out—

CALONICE:
By Zeus, that's best, as far as we're concerned—

LYSISTRATA:
And the Boeotians with them, root and branch—[4]   35

CALONICE:
All of them, fine, except those gorgeous eels.[5]

LYSISTRATA:
I won't say Athens, since the omen's bad.
Imagine if I'd said it—shocking, huh?
If all the women come together here—
Boeotians, Peloponnesians, and the rest—   40
And us—together we can salvage Greece.

CALONICE:
What thoughtful thing could women ever do?
What vivid venture? We just sit decked out
In saffron gowns, makeup about this thick,
Cimberian[6] lingerie, and platform shoes.   45

---

4. The Peloponnesians and the Boeotians were the chief enemies of Athens during the Peloponnesian War.

5. The eels from Lake Copaïs were a culinary export sorely missed during the war, when trade restrictions were in force.

6. May refer to the Crimean region; in any case, the clothing is exotic.

LYSISTRATA:
It's those that I intend to save our race:
Those dresses, and perfume, and rouge, and shoes,
And little see-through numbers that we wear.

CALONICE:
How's that?

LYSISTRATA:
                    The men surviving won't lift up
50   Their spears (against each other, anyway).

CALONICE:
By the Two Gods,[7] I've got a dress to dye!

LYSISTRATA:
Or shields—

CALONICE:
                    I've got a negligée to try!

LYSISTRATA:
Or knives—

CALONICE:
                    Ooh, ooh, and shoes! And shoes to buy!

LYSISTRATA:
So shouldn't all the other women come?

CALONICE:
55   Well, YES! With wings to boost them, hours ago!

LYSISTRATA:
It's such a bitch assembling Attica.[8]
You know they'd rather die than be on time.
Nobody even came here from the coast,
Or out of Salamis.[9]

---

7. Demeter and Kore.

8. The whole region of Attica, not the city of Athens alone, was the relevant political unit, with rural dwellers having equal rights. Political assemblies in Athens encompassed all of the demes, or administrative areas.

9. Key strategic areas, with special political significance. See also line 411 and note.

CALONICE:

I'm sure they got
Up on those mounts of theirs[10] at break of day.   60

LYSISTRATA:

I thought it would be only logical
For the Acharnians to start the crowd,[11]
But they're not here yet.

CALONICE:

Well, Theogenes' wife
Has raised her glass to us—any excuse.[12]
No, wait. Look thataway: here come a few.   65

LYSISTRATA:

And now a couple more.

> *(Several women straggle in, among them Myrrhine, a
> young and beautiful matron.)*

CALONICE:

Yuck, what a smell!
Where are they from?

LYSISTRATA:

The puke-bush swamp.

CALONICE:

By Zeus,
It must be quite a place to raise a stink.[13]

---

10. Literally, "straddled the yachts" or "mounted astride horses," with a joke on a sexual position with the woman on top.

11. The deme of Acharnae had been repeatedly and particularly badly ravaged by the invading Spartan army earlier in the war, while its inhabitants stayed in Athens for safety. In Aristophanes' play *Acharnians*, the chorus is a group of old men from this deme, first opposing peace but then won over.

12. A puzzling pair of lines. This Theogenes has not been firmly identified. His wife either "consulted [the goddess] Hecate" about coming, or "lifted her sail/wine cup."

13. The deme of Anagyrus was swampy and full of a malodorous bush that gave its name to the place. "To shake the anagyros" meant to cause trouble.

MYRRHINE:[14]
    Ooh, Lysistrata, are we very late?
    Too mad to say?

LYSISTRATA:
70   Why should I not be mad?
    This is important! Why not come on time?

MYRRHINE:
    Well, it was dark—I couldn't find my thing—[15]
    But say what's on your mind, now that we're here.

LYSISTRATA:
    No, wait a little while. The other wives,
75   The Boeotians and the Peloponnesians,
    Are on the way.

MYRRHINE:
              All right, of course we'll wait.
    Look over there, though—that's not Lampito[16]?

> *(Enter Lampito, a strapping woman in a distinct,*
> *more revealing costume. Several others in various*
> *foreign dress accompany her, including a Boeotian*
> *and a Corinthian Woman.)*

LYSISTRATA:
    Darling Laconian, Lampito, hail!
    How I admire your gleaming gorgeousness,
80   Your radiant skin, your body sleek and plump.
    I bet that you could choke a bull.[17]

LAMPITO:
                  I could.
    I'm in such shape I kick my own sweet ass.[18]

---

14. Probably something like "Bearded Clam."

15. Literally, "little belt," possibly an undergarment.

16. From the word for "shining," or "light."

17. Spartan women were more active than their counterparts in Athens and even exercised in public. Their health must indeed have been better than that of women mostly confined to their homes.

18. A Spartan dance involved jumping and slapping one's own soles against the buttocks.

CALONICE: *(Prodding curiously.)*
  And what a brace of boobs. How bountiful!

LAMPITO:
  What am I s'pposed to be? A pig for sale?[19]

LYSISTRATA:
  And what's this other young thing's origin?   85

LAMPITO:
  Boeotia sent her as a delegate.
  She's at your service.

MYRRHINE: *(Peeking under woman's clothes.)*
                    Boeotian—sure enough:
  Just look at what a broad and fertile plain.

CALONICE: *(Peeking likewise.)*
  She's even pulled the weeds.[20] Now *that* is class.

LYSISTRATA:
  And what's the other girl?

LAMPITO:

                    Corinthian.   90
  Hell, ain't she fine?

LYSISTRATA:

                    Damn right she's fine . . . from here,
  And get another angle on her—wow!

LAMPITO:
  We're like a women's army. Who put out
  The word to assemble?

LYSISTRATA:

                    That was me.

LAMPITO:

                              How come?
  Tell us what's going on.

---

19. Literally, "You finger me like a sacrificial victim." An animal offered to a god had to be a perfect specimen.

20. "Pennyroyal," a characteristic Boeotian plant, could also mean "pubic hair." Careful female grooming included plucking or burning pubic hair into some tidy shape.

CALONICE:

95   Yeah, honey, what?
 What all-important burr is up your butt?

LYSISTRATA:
 The time has come. But first you answer me
 One weensy little thing.

CALONICE:

        Okay. Just ask.

LYSISTRATA:
 I know you all have husbands far from home
100 On active service. Don't you miss the men,
 The fathers of your children, all this time?

CALONICE:
 My husband's been away five months in Thrace.
 Somebody's gotta watch the general.[21]

MYRRHINE:
 Mine's been in Pylos[22] seven freaking months.

LAMPITO:
105 Once in a while, mine's back, but then he's off.
 It's like that shield's a friggin' pair of wings.

LYSISTRATA:
 And since the Milesians deserted us[23]
 (Along with every scrap of lover here),
 We've even lost those six-inch substitutes,
110 Those dinky dildos for emergencies.
 If I could find a way to end this war,
 Would you be willing partners?

---

21. "Guarding Eucrates," probably the brother of the general Nicias, who had played a dismal role in the Sicilian expedition. Nothing further about Eucrates' circumstances is known.

22. A fortified coastal city in the Peloponnese, which Athens had occupied since 425 B.C.E.

23. Miletus revolted from the Delian League, or Athenian empire, in 412 B.C.E., the year before the first production of *Lysistrata*. Dildos were apparently one of Miletus' exports.

CALONICE:

         I sure would.
I'd sacrifice my nicest dress to buy
Some wine (and sacrifice the wine to me).

MYRRHINE:

 I'd cut myself in two and donate half—   115
 A flat slice like a bottom-feeding fish.

LAMPITO:

 I'd hike clear up Mount Taygetus[24] to see
 If peace is flashin' somewhere way far off.

LYSISTRATA:

 Fine. So. Here goes. You need to know the plan.
 Yes, ladies. How we force the men to peace.   120
 How are we going to do it? We must all
 Hold off—

CALONICE:

    From *what?*

LYSISTRATA:

       You're positive you will?

CALONICE:

 We'll do it! Even if it costs our lives.

LYSISTRATA:

 From now on, no more penises for you.

  (The women begin to disperse.)

 Wait! You can't all just turn and walk away!   125
 And what's this purse-lipped shaking of your heads?
 You're turning pale—is that a tear I see?
 Will you or not? You can't hold out on me!

CALONICE:

 No, I don't think so. Let the war go on.

MYRRHINE:

 Me? Not a chance in hell, so screw the war.   130

---

24. Near Sparta.

LYSISTRATA:
    That's it, my piscine heroine? You said
    Just now that you'd bisect yourself for peace.

CALONICE:
    ANYTHING else for me. I'd walk through fire,
    But do without a dick? Be serious!
135   There's nothing, Lysistrata, like a dick.

LYSISTRATA: *(Turning to Woman #1.)*
    And you?

WOMAN #1:
            Me? Mmm, I'll take the fire, thanks.

LYSISTRATA:
    Oh, gender fit for boning up the butt!25
    No wonder we're the stuff of tragedies:
    Some guy, a bit of nookie, and a brat.26

            (To Lampito.)

140   But you, sweet foreigner, if you alone
    Stand with me, then we still could save the day.
    Give me your vote!

LAMPITO:
                    Shit, it's no easy thing
    To lie in bed alone without no dong . . .
    But count me in. Peace we just gotta have.

LYSISTRATA:
16   The only *woman* in this half-assed horde!

CALONICE:
    Suppose we did—the thing you say we should—
    Which gods forbid—what has that got to do
    With peace?

---

25. A nearly literal translation. Anal sex was associated with shame-lessness.

26. Literally, "Poseidon and a skiff." In a lost play of Sophocles, the heroine Tyro is seduced by the sea god Poseidon. Her twin sons, Pelias and Neleus, are set adrift in a small boat but rescued and eventually reunited with her.

LYSISTRATA:
>   A lot, I promise you. If we
> Sit in our quarters, powdered daintily,
> As good as nude in those imported slips,
> And—just—slink by, with crotches nicely groomed,[27]
> The men will swell right up and want to boink,
> But we won't let them near us, we'll refuse—
> Trust me, they'll make a treaty at a dash.

150

LAMPITO:
> You're right! You know how Menelaus saw
> Helen's bazooms and threw his weapon down.[28]

155

CALONICE:
> But what if they just shrug and walk away?

LYSISTRATA:
> For them, there's just one place a dildo fits.[29]

CALONICE:
> As if a fake is lots of fun for us.
> Suppose they grab us, drag us into bed.
> We'll have no choice.

160

LYSISTRATA:
>   Resist. Hang on the door.

CALONICE:
> Suppose they beat us.

LYSISTRATA:
>   Yield a lousy lay.
> They force a woman, and it's no more fun.
> Plus, no more housework! They'll give up—you'll see
> How fast. No husband's going to like to screw
> Unless he knows his woman likes it too.

165

---

27. See line 89 and note.

28. In one version of the myth, Menelaus intended to kill his wife when he got her back after the fall of Troy but was overcome by her beauty.

29. This is the best I could do with a line based on a literary allusion for which we have little context: "Do what Pherecrates [a comic playwright] says/does, and skin the skinned bitch," orders Lysistrata. The metaphor is thought to have referred to frustration and hopelessness, and here somehow plays comically on the idea of leather dildos.

CALONICE:
>If that's the thing you're set on, fine—okay.

LAMPITO:
>We'll force the Spartan husbands into peace:
>No cheating, quibbling, squabbling any more.[30]
>But what about them lowlifes in your town?
>What'll you do so they don't run amok?[31]

170

LYSISTRATA:
>We'll handle things on our side. Don't you fret.

LAMPITO:
>I will. You know that god of yours has got
>An expense account for sails and all the rest.[32]

LYSISTRATA:
>We've put aside that obstacle ourselves.
>Today we occupy the citadel.
>This is the mission of the senior squad.
>While we confer here, they've gone up to fake
>A sacrifice and storm the Acropolis.

175

LAMPITO:
>You *are* a clever thang. Fine all around!

180

LYSISTRATA:
>Let's quickly swear an oath, my friend, and set
>Our concord up unbendable as bronze.[33]

---

30. The Spartans had a reputation for sharp dealing. This obloquy in the mouth of a Spartan wife is not dramatically plausible, but the Athenian audience must have enjoyed it.

31. The Athenian lower classes, from which the navy's rowers were drawn, tended to support the war that provided them with work, pay, and prestige. Also, the navy was the basis of the lucrative empire that provided pork-barrel benefits for all Athenian citizens, especially the poor.

32. On the fortified and magnificently built up Acropolis, under the authority of the goddess Athena, was the treasury of the Delian League, which financed Athens' war effort. Even when virtually besieged by land, Athens continued to enforce revenue collection by sea.

33. The following scene is a parody of men's oath ceremonies. For peace agreements, wine and not a slaughtered beast sanctified the words. For the wrong reasons, the women are about to make the right choice.

LAMPITO:
Give us whatever oath you wanna give.

LYSISTRATA:
So where's the guard? (I'm talking to you! Wake up!)[34]

(Enter Female Scythian Guard in an exotic uniform.)

Bring here your shield and set it upside down. 185

(She obeys. The women pause.)

Now where's the sacrifice?

CALONICE:
What can we find
To swear on, Lysistrata?

LYSISTRATA:
Aeschylus
Had people drain the blood of slaughtered sheep
Into a shield.[35]

CALONICE:
A shield? To swear for peace?
Excuse me, honey, but that can't be right. 190

LYSISTRATA:
What else, then?

CALONICE:
We could find a giant stud,
A pure white stallion, say, and hack him up.

LYSISTRATA:
What do you mean, a horse?[36]

CALONICE:
We need to swear

---

34. The local security force in Athens consisted mainly of foreign archers, slaves generically referred to as "Scythians." Lysistrata summons a "Scythianess," the (to the Athenians) ludicrous female version of a policeman.

35. Based on a line from Aeschylus' *Seven against Thebes.*

36. Scholars do not know, either. There may be some kind of joke here, with "white horse" standing for a penis.

On *something*.

LYSISTRATA:
                    Listen up! I know the way:
195   A big black drinking bowl laid on its back;
         A jar of Thasian to sacrifice;
         An oath to mix no water with the wine.[37]

LAMPITO:
Shit sakes, I like that more than I can say.

LYSISTRATA:
Somebody bring a jar out, and a bowl.

         (The items are brought.)

MYRRHINE:
200   Hey, sisters, that's some massive pottery!

CALONICE: *(Snatching.)*
Just fondling it, you'd start to feel real good.

LYSISTRATA:
Put the bowl down and help me hold the beast.[38]

         *(Calonice relinquishes her hold. All the women join in
         lifting the jar.)*

Holy Persuasion, and our Bowl for Pals,
Be gracious toward this women's sacrifice.

         (Lysistrata opens the jar. The women pour.)

CALONICE:
205   Propitiously the gleaming blood spurts forth!

LAMPITO:
By Castor,[39] and it smells real pretty too.

---

37. Drinking unmixed wine was a fairly extreme indulgence. Even at men's drinking parties, which could easily end in orgies, water was poured into the wine in fixed proportions.

38. The jar; the sacrificial animal was handled in a prescribed manner.

39. Castor and Polydeuces, twin sons of Zeus, were demigods important in Sparta.

MYRRHINE:
Girls, let me be the first to swear the oath.[40]

CALONICE:
No way, by Aphrodite. We'll draw lots.

LYSISTRATA:
Grip the bowl's rim, Lampito and the rest.

> *(They obey.)*

One of you, speak for all, repeat my words,   210
Then everybody else confirm the oath.
Neither my boyfriend nor my wedded spouse—

CALONICE:
Neither my boyfriend nor my wedded spouse—

LYSISTRATA:
Shall touch me when inflated. Say it, girl!

CALONICE:
Shall touch me when inflated. Holy hell!   215
Knees—Lysistrata—wobbly. Gonna faint!

LYSISTRATA: *(Sternly, ignoring this distress.)*
I shall stay home unhumped both night and day,

CALONICE:
I shall stay home unhumped both night and day,

LYSISTRATA:
While wearing makeup and a flashy dress,

CALONICE:
While wearing makeup and a flashy dress,   220

LYSISTRATA:
That I may give my man the scorching hots,

CALONICE:
That I may give my man the scorching hots,

LYSISTRATA:
But I will not consent to what he wants,

---

40. The first to swear would also be the first to drink.

CALONICE:
But I will not consent to what he wants,

LYSISTRATA:
225   And if he forces me, against my will,

CALONICE:
And if he forces me, against my will,

LYSISTRATA:
Then I will sulk, I will not hump along;

CALONICE:
Then I will sulk, I will not hump along;

LYSISTRATA:
I will not point my slippers at the roof;

CALONICE:
230   I will not point my slippers at the roof;

LYSISTRATA:
Nor, like a lion knickknack, ass in air—

CALONICE:
Nor, like a lion knickknack, ass in air—[41]

LYSISTRATA:
Abiding by these vows, may I drink wine;

CALONICE:
Abiding by these vows, may I drink wine;

LYSISTRATA:
235   If I transgress, let water fill the bowl.

CALONICE:
If I transgress, let water fill the bowl.

LYSISTRATA:
Now do you all consent?

ALL:
By Zeus, we do.

---

41. Literally, "I will not assume the position of a lioness on a cheese grater." Ornamental lions were typically depicted set to pounce, crouching in front but with their hindquarters raised.

LYSISTRATA:
I dedicate this bowl. *(She drinks heartily.)*

CALONICE:
Just drink your share!
We've got to work together, starting now.

(All drink. A mass ululation is heard offstage.)

LAMPITO:
Somebody's shouting.

LYSISTRATA:
As I said before: 240
It's our contingent on the citadel.
They've taken it already. Lampito,
You go arrange things back in Sparta. These

(Indicates Spartan Women.)

Will need to stay with us as hostages.[42]
We'll join the rest of the Athenians 245
And help them heave the bars behind the doors.

CALONICE:
You think the men will find out right away
And all gang up on us?

LYSISTRATA:
The hell with them.
They can't make threats or fires fierce enough.
These doors stay shut. We only open them 250
On those exact conditions we've set down.

CALONICE:
So Aphrodite help us, we'll stay put,
Or not deserve the cherished title "Bitch."

(All the women exit into stage building.)

(Enter a Chorus of twelve Old Men, carrying logs, unlit torches, and pots of burning charcoal.)

---

42. It was a normal precaution to keep hostages to ensure compliance with an international agreement.

MEN'S CHORUS LEADER:
> Draces, lead on, ignore your throbbing back
255 > Under the fresh, green weight of olive trunks.

CHORUS OF OLD MEN:
> A long life brings lots
> That's surprising to see.
> This, Strumodorus, is a new one on me.
260 > At our expense
> This pestilence
> Festered at home indoors.
> They've taken our citadel!
> Athena's image as well![43]
265 > They've barred the ceremonial gates,[44] the whores!

MEN'S CHORUS LEADER:
> Straight ahead is the fortress, Philurgus.
> To pile up one pyre and set it afire
> For all with a hand in this wicked affair
> Can pass without debate or amendments
270 > Or special pleading—well, first get Lycon's wife.[45]

CHORUS OF OLD MEN:
> Demeter's my witness, this stunt isn't cute.
> Like Cleomenes, these girls won't find it a hoot.
> Cocky Spartan! He went away,
275 > Dealt with efficiently, let's say,
> His arms surrendered. He wore a crappy trace
> Of the clothes that he came in.
> He was blasted with famine,
280 > With six hard years of beard and crud on his face.

MEN'S CHORUS LEADER:
> Fierce was the siege that we sat for the bastard,
> Camping in seventeen ranks at the bulwark.[46]

---

43. An ancient wooden statue of Athena.

44. The Propylaea, a massive structure through which important processions passed.

45. Lycon was a prominent politician whose wife had a reputation for promiscuity.

46. A gross exaggeration of a brief seizure of the Acropolis by a Spartan king in 508 B.C.E.—much too early for the speakers to have played any part.

But the gods and Euripides both detest women.[47]
I'll cram their impertinence straight back inside—
If I don't, take my Marathon monument down.[48]   285

CHORUS OF OLD MEN:
The cliff in the road
Where I haul my load
Is right before me, I have come so fast.
Too bad—no mule!
So much to pull.   290
Literally, this is a pain in the ass.
But I won't tire—
I'll puff the fire—
Won't get distracted—it's got to last!

(*They blow, recoil.*)

Oh shit, the smoke!
I'm going to choke!   295

From the basin where it slept,
Lord Hercules, how savagely it leapt,
Like a rabid bitch, to bite me in the eyes.
It's Lemnian, I think,
From the land where women stink.[49]
It reeks of everything that I despise.
Up to the heights!
Defend our rights!
The goddess needs us, don't you realize?

(*They blow, recoil.*)

Oh hell, the ash!
I'm going to crash!   305

---

47. The tragedian Euripides' searing depictions of rebellious women made him a frequent comic butt as a misogynist.

48. To have fought against the Persians at the Battle of Marathon in 490 B.C.E., these men would have to be about a hundred years old.

49. In a myth unaccountably never exploited by the advertisers of feminine deodorants, Aphrodite punished the women of Lemnos, who had neglected her rites, by inflicting a foul odor on them. They then murdered their disgusted and defecting husbands. Lemnos also had certain geological and ritual associations with fire. The passage contains an untranslatable pun on the word for the pus from sore eyes.

MEN'S CHORUS LEADER:
  Gods answer our prayers and the fire rears high.
  Assignment The First: put the logs on the ground.
  Here are some torches to ram in the brazier.
  Rush then, and batter yourselves on the gates.
310 Call for surrender. A slit should spread open.
  Otherwise, light the gates, smoke the broads out.
  Put down your logs, men. (This smoke is a hassle!)
  The generals in Samos are shirking the work.[50]

      (He heaves his wood down.)

  That's better—the load has stopped warping my back.
315 This bucket of coals has the task to provide
  Me—hey, me first!—with a virulent torch.
  Great goddess Victory,[51] give me a prize[52]
  For feminine insolence valiantly squished.

      (The men busy themselves with lighting torches.)

      *(A Chorus of twelve Old Women enter from the
      opposite side, carrying water jars.)*

WOMEN'S CHORUS LEADER:
  Women, that bright thing in a murky cloud—
320 Is it a fire? Quick, let's get on the scene.

CHORUS OF OLD WOMEN:
  Nicodice, hurry!
  Calyce's getting lit!
  Critylla's getting buffeted
  By blazing winds
325 And old men full of shit.
  Oh, dear! Oh, my! Am I too late?
  I went at dawn to wrangle free this water.
  I struggled through the crash and screech and slaughter—
  Elbows flailing, jars askew—

---

50. The Athenian navy was based at Samos during this period.

51. Athena Nike (Victory) had a temple to the right of those entering
the Propylaea.

52. "A trophy," which for the Greeks was a tree or post with the
enemy's arms hung on it.

Scurvy maids, slaves with tattoos—[53]   330
In a panic raised this urn,
Downright manic to return
To keep my friends from getting singed.
I heard the news about unhinged
Codgers who, like lumberjacks,[54]   335
Dumped their logs in ten-ton stacks
And launched the most
Outrageous boasts.
They said they'd make ashes of living profanity.   340
Help, Goddess, save women from such inhumanity,
And they will restore your dear nation to sanity.
That's why, O Golden-Helmeted One,
They dared to occupy your throne.   345
Oh, be their ally, Triton's daughter.[55]
Zap every spark out with this water.
Help us haul it to the top.
What these beasts are doing must stop!

(The women notice the men and their equipment.)

WOMEN'S CHORUS LEADER:
Wait! What can this be? They've been busy pricks.   350
Is this the work of conscientious citizens—or dicks?

(The men notice the women.)

MEN'S CHORUS LEADER:
We didn't reckon on this other swarm
Of women, rushing toward the gates to help.

WOMEN'S CHORUS LEADER:
What are you scared of? Do we seem a throng?
You're looking at just .01 percent.   355

MEN'S CHORUS LEADER:
Impossible to let them blather on!

---

53. A runaway or other criminal slave might be punished with tattoo-ing or branding.

54. "As if to heat a bath" with wood as the fuel.

55. All three references in the women's prayer are to Athena. She has a "golden crest" on her helmet. The last reference is obscure; Athena was normally said to have been born from the head of Zeus.

We'd better whack them with this wood instead.

WOMEN'S CHORUS LEADER:
Girls, put your pitchers down, out of the way,
So if they lift a hand, we'll be prepared.

MEN'S CHORUS LEADER:
360   If somebody had done a proper job
Of slapping them, they'd keep their yappers shut.[56]

WOMEN'S CHORUS LEADER:
Fine. Try it. Here's a cheek for you to smack.
And then I'll tear your balls off like a bitch.

MEN'S CHORUS LEADER:
Shut up! I'll pound you hollow if you don't.

WOMEN'S CHORUS LEADER:
365   Just put a fingertip on Stratyllis—

MEN'S CHORUS LEADER:
And if I pummel her? What will you do?

WOMEN'S CHORUS LEADER:
I'll gnaw your lungs and claw your entrails out.

MEN'S CHORUS LEADER:
Euripides is my authority
On women: "She's a creature lacking shame."[57]

WOMEN'S CHORUS LEADER:
370   Honey, we'd better lift these jars again.

MEN'S CHORUS LEADER:
What did you bring the water for, you scum?

WOMEN'S CHORUS LEADER:
And what's the fire for, you senile coots?
Fogies flambés?

---

56. The lines refer to Bupalus as an assault victim. He was a sixth-century B.C.E. sculptor who feuded with the poet Hipponax and committed suicide because of the violently abusive verse directed at him. The allusion is an excellent one to illustrate a fight that will turn out to be mostly verbal.

57. See line 283 and note. Here Aristophanes may be quoting directly from a tragedy.

His dancing dame yelled, "Poor Adonis!" He
Moved that we try Zacynthus[65] for recruits.
Feeling no pain, the woman on the tiles　　　　395
Burped, "Mourn Adonis!" And Demostratus
Blasted along, that psycho.[66] This is what
Happens because of women on the loose.[67]

MEN'S CHORUS LEADER:
No kidding. What about the women here?
They've even emptied pitchers on our heads,　　400
Washed us against our will. Our cloaks are drenched.
You'd think that we were all incontinent.

COUNCILOR:
Briny Poseidon, that's what we deserve,
Conniving with our wives the way we do,
Drawing them diagrams for decadence—　　　405
Of course they sprout conspiracies like this.
We stride into a jeweler's and we say,
"Goldsmith, the necklace that you made my wife—
She was, uh, dancing—hard—the other night.
The prong—you know—got jiggled and fell out.　410
I have to sail to Salamis today,[68]
But if you're free this evening, go around
And put that thing back in, and screw it tight."
Or at a leather workshop someone asks
A strapping, really well-equipped young man,　　415
"Oh, Mister Shoemaker, you know my wife's
Little toe, and how tender it can get,

---

65. An island to the west of Greece, allied to Athens.

66. An untranslatable pun on Demostratus' family name.

67. The Greeks were highly superstitious. After many of their young men died in the disastrous Sicilian expedition (launched in 415 B.C.E.), an Athenian might well recall the bad omen of a woman heard mourning for a beautiful young man while the Assembly heard proposals for the expedition. But Aristophanes' target is the self-righteous silliness of the speaker, who, we can tell by an easy read between the lines, supported the expedition himself. He blames the disaster chiefly on one drunken woman, rather than on the people who sold citizens a terrible idea, or on the citizens who bought it.

68. "Sailing to Salamis" probably had a sexual meaning.

Rubbed by her sandal strap? Drop by at noon
And give her hole a jimmy and a stretch."
420   No wonder it's resulted in *this* mess.
I AM A COUNCILOR. It is my JOB
To find the wood for oars and PAY FOR IT.
And now these WOMEN shut the gates on me!
It's no good standing here. Those crowbars, quick!
425   I'll separate these women from their gall.

(A slave is indecisive.)

Hey, slack-jaw, move! What are you waiting for?
You're looking for a pub where you can hide?
Both of you, put these levers in the gates
From that side, and from here I'll stick mine in
And help you shove.

(Lysistrata emerges from the stage building.)

LYSISTRATA:
430   Right, you can shove those bars.
It doesn't take a tool to bring me out.
You don't need siege equipment here. Just brains.

COUNCILOR:
Really, you walking poo? Where *is* that guard?
Grab her and tie her hands behind her back.

LYSISTRATA:
435   By Artemis, if that state property's
Fingertip touches me, I'll make him wail.

(Guard backs away.)

COUNCILOR:
You're scared of her? Grab her around the waist,
And you—look sharp and help him tie her hands.

(Old Woman #1 enters from door.)

OLD WOMAN #1:
Pandrosus[69] help me. Lay one cuticle
440   On her, and I shall beat you till you shit.

(The two guards slink off.)

---

69. An Athenian princess of myth.

COUNCILOR:
Such language! Where'd the other archer go?
Get this one first. Just hear that potty mouth!

(Old Woman #2 enters from door.)

OLD WOMAN #2:
By Phosphorus,[70] one hangnail grazes her,
And you'll be nursing eyes as black as tar.

(Third guard retreats.)

COUNCILOR:
What *is* this? Where's a guard? Get hold of her!   445
One little expedition's at an end.

(Old Woman #3 enters from door.)

OLD WOMAN #3:
Go near her, by Tauropolus,[71] and I
Will give you screaming lessons on your hair.

(Fourth guard makes himself scarce.)

COUNCILOR:
Now I'm in deep. I've got no archers left.
We can't let women have the final stomp!   445
Scythians, we must form a battle line
And march straight at them.

*(Guards reluctantly gather together again from
a distance.)*

LYSISTRATA:
                        You'll find out, I swear,
That we've got four divisions tucked away,
Heavy-armed women itching for a fight.

COUNCILOR:
Attendants, twist their arms behind their backs.   455

(The guards advance.)

---

70. An epithet of Hecate and Artemis, "Light-Bearer."
71. Artemis, an epithet perhaps meaning "Drawn in a Cart by a Bull."

LYSISTRATA:
Thunder out, allied women, from the walls!
Sellers of garlic, gruel, and poppy seeds,
Greengrocers, bakers, landladies—attack!
Yank them and shove them! Sock them! Hammer them!
460   Insult, belittle them—get really coarse!

> (*A mob of women enters and descends on the guards
> with physical and verbal abuse.*)

Fall back! To strip their dignity's enough.[72]

> (*The women retreat. The guards lie flattened
> and immobile.*)

COUNCILOR:
My bodyguard reduced to diddly-squat!

LYSISTRATA:
But what were you expecting? Facing troops?
Or herding slaves? Apparently you don't
Think we have guts.

COUNCILOR:
465   The female gut's quite deep:
I've seen the way that you perform in bars.

MEN'S CHORUS LEADER:
Hey you, our Councilor: you're wasting words
By arguing with wild things like a fool.
They didn't even let us get undressed,
470   But bathed us without benefit of soap.

WOMEN'S CHORUS LEADER:
Well, you, sir, think your fellow citizens
Are fit for bullying. You *want* black eyes?
Given the choice, I'd play a prim, demure
Young girl, disturbing no one by so much
475   As blinking. I'm a hornet when I'm roused.

CHORUS OF OLD MEN:
O, Zeus, what shall we do with these vermin?

---

72. "Do not strip [their armor]," orders Lysistrata, like a general giving
a command to abstain from plunder.

We can't just take it. Let's examine
How it happened,
Why these women
Plotted to snatch the bouldered shrine,   480
Out of bounds, high in the air,
The Acropolis,
And make it theirs.

MEN'S CHORUS LEADER: *(To Councilor.)*
Challenge, refute! Whatever sounds right must be wrong!
If they shortchange us, it's the ultimate disgrace.   485

COUNCILOR:
Right. Question Number One: I am anxious to hear
Your motivation for barring the fortress doors.

LYSISTRATA:
Keeping the money here will starve the war to death.

COUNCILOR:
Money—and war? Huh?

LYSISTRATA:
                    There's a rats' nest in this town.
Pisander[73] and his public office-stalking ilk   490
Raised hell—it yielded marvelous chances to steal.
Who gives a hoot what they do now? The money's safe.

COUNCILOR:
And *your* plan is—?

LYSISTRATA:
                    You have to ask? It's *management.*

COUNCILOR:
Of public funds? By *you?*

LYSISTRATA:
                    And what's so strange in that?
You let us women do the budgeting at home.   495

COUNCILOR:
It's not the same at all!

---

73. He actually helped lead a briefly successful coup later in 411 B.C.E.

LYSISTRATA:
                         Because—?

COUNCILOR:
                                    You don't fight wars!

LYSISTRATA:
    And you don't have to either.

COUNCILOR:
                                    We're in jeopardy!

LYSISTRATA:
    We'll save you.

COUNCILOR:
                    You?

LYSISTRATA:
                         Yeah, us.

COUNCILOR:
                         But that's unthinkable.

LYSISTRATA:
    Think what you like.

COUNCILOR:
                         Unutterable.

LYSISTRATA:
                                    No, uttered.
    It doesn't matter how you feel.

COUNCILOR:
500   THIS ISN'T RIGHT!

LYSISTRATA:
    Too bad.

COUNCILOR:
            BUT I DON'T WANT IT!

LYSISTRATA:
                                    Then you need it more.

COUNCILOR:
    How can you meddle in the stern affairs of state?

LYSISTRATA:
  Listen here—

COUNCILOR:
  The hand may be quicker than the mouth.

LYSISTRATA:
  Listen! And keep a grip on your hands.

COUNCILOR:
  Can't manage.
  I'm furious!

WOMAN #1:
  And what you're *going* to be is *sore*.   505

COUNCILOR:
  No, *you'll* be sore, old buzzard! *(To Lysistrata.)* You, go on.

LYSISTRATA:
  I will.
  Throughout this futile war, we women held our peace.
  Propriety (and husbands) permitted no peep
  To escape our mouths. But we weren't exactly pleased.
  We did hear how things were going. When you had passed   510
  Some subnormally thought-out, doom-laden decree,
  We'd say, aching, but on the surface simpering,
  "What rider to the treaty did you decide on
  Today at the Assembly?"[74] "That's not your affair!
  Shut up." And lo, I did shut up.

OLD WOMAN #1:
  I wouldn't have.   515

COUNCILOR:
  We'd have clocked you if you didn't.

LYSISTRATA:
  That's why I did.
  Another day we'd ask, about some even more
  Malignant move, "Do you *ever* think first, big boy?"

---

74. In 418 B.C.E, an important treaty engraved on a stele (stone col-
umn) was altered by an inscription saying that the Spartans had broken
the treaty. This was obviously a provocative statement to incorporate
into a public monument.

He'd glare, order me back to my wool and warn
520   That I could soon be wailing. *"Men* will see to the war."

COUNCILOR:
And right he was, by Zeus.

LYSISTRATA:
                       You worthless loser, why?
Because ineptitude's a shield against advice?
It got so you were yakking in the streets yourselves:
"We've got no *men* left in the country." "Yeah, no fake."
525   Hearing stuff like that, we decided women would
Muster and deliver Greece. Why piddle around?
We've got some useful things to tell you. If you stay
Quiet the way *we* always did, we'll set you straight.

COUNCILOR:
Insufferably presumptuous notion!

LYSISTRATA:
                       SHUT UP!!

COUNCILOR:
530   Shut up for you, abomination in a veil!
I'd sooner perish.

LYSISTRATA:
             So you're hung up on the veil?

*(The Councilor is mobbed and outfitted as a
housewife.)*

Hang one on yourself. Try mine.
Drape it around your skull.
Sit on this chair. Don't whine!

OLD WOMAN #1:
535   Hike up your skirt, card gobs of wool
Into a basket on the floor.

LYSISTRATA:
Look dumb. Chew gum.[75]
The women will deal with the war.

---

75. The Greeks chewed beans instead of tree sap, but otherwise the
practice was similar.

WOMEN'S CHORUS LEADER:
Leave your pitchers, women, leap up.
Friends are struggling, we must keep up.   540

I will never tire of dancing.
Waking strength will move my feet.
I'll accept the worst ordeals.
What's so fine as to compete   545
With these women's sense and valor,
With their charm and civic zeal?

Grannies on the go, mommies with mucho macho,
The wind is behind your rage, so harden, advance!   550

LYSISTRATA:
If the Cyprian Goddess[76] and sweet Eros breathe
Desire through us till our thighs and bosoms steam,
Thereby equipping men with feel-good weaponry,
The Greeks will rename us *Anti*-Battle-Axes![77]

COUNCILOR
What are you going to do?

LYSISTRATA:
                              Well, first of all, we'll stop   555
Those kooks who go shopping in battle gear.

OLD WOMAN #1:
                                          Hell, yes!

LYSISTRATA:
They haul an armory among the pottery
And greens, and bash around—it's like some goddamn cult.[78]

COUNCILOR:
They're dedicated men!

LYSISTRATA:
                          No, dedicated dweebs.

---

76. Aphrodite.

77. Literally, "Lysimaches." See note 1.

78. "Like Corybantes"—ecstatic dancers with noisy armor. They were
a byword for the mentally unstable.

560   They heft their doughty Gorgon shields[79] and buy sardines.

OLD WOMAN #1:
A captain, streaming-haired, aloft upon his steed,
Proffered a bronze hat to be shoveled full of soup.
A Thracian—just like Tereus![80]—clattered his shield
And downed forthwith the figs of the routed vendor.

COUNCILOR:
But there's a perfect pandemonium worldwide.
565   How would you cope?

LYSISTRATA:
                                    Without a lot of strain.

COUNCILOR:
                                                    What?! How?

LYSISTRATA:
Say that the wool's a mass of tangles. Take it thus,

   (Miming throughout.)

Draw it apart with spindles—make some sense of it.
That's how we'll loosen up this war—if we're allowed.
570   Ambassadors are spindles—they can sort it out.

COUNCILOR:
Spindles and gobs of wool—it's just too fatuous.
We're in a crisis.

LYSISTRATA:
                        With a modicum of smarts,
You'd copy the administration of our wool.

COUNCILOR:
Do tell me how.

LYSISTRATA:
                        First, give the fleece a bath to dunk

---

79. The Gorgon was a mythological creature with a woman's face and snakes for hair. She was said to turn everyone who saw her into stone, so her image was a natural one to appear on shields.

80. A savage Thracian king of myth; see note 112. Thracians were thought of as semibarbarians, and Thracian mercenaries must have been fairly conspicuous in Athens.

Away the sheep dung. Spread your city on a bed 575
Next, and beat out all the layabouts and briars.
Then card out any clumps—you know, the cliques of chumps,
Magistracy-mongers.[81] Pluck their little heads off.
Comb what's left into a single goodwill basket.
Wad in your resident aliens and other 580
Nice foreigners, and don't leave out public debtors.
And heck, as for the city's scattered colonies,
I want you to construe them as neglected tufts,
Each on its lonesome. Gather them all together,
Bunch them up tight, and finally you'll have one 585
Big ball. Use it to weave the city something fine.

COUNCILOR:
Wads and rods and balls—the paradigm's atrocious!
What have you got to do with war?

LYSISTRATA:
                                    You scrap of scum,
We fight it twice: it's we who give the hoplites life,
And then we send them off, for you—

COUNCILOR:
                                    That spot is sore![82] 590

LYSISTRATA:
Us young and frisky females, who must seize the night,
War puts to bed beside ourselves. But screw us wives:
I ache for the girls turned crones and never married.

COUNCILOR:
Don't men get old?

LYSISTRATA:
                    You *know* it's nothing like the same!
Any decrepit veteran, no questions asked, 595
Can get a child-bride, but a woman's chance is zip
After her prime. She sits there maiming daisies—crap![83]

---

81. Oligarchic clubs. See lines 490–1 and Commentary 1, page 82.
82. Probably refers to the Sicilian expedition. See note 67.
83. "She sits, looking for omens."

COUNCILOR:
As long as men can get it up—

LYSISTRATA:
Why don't you die and shut it up?

(*The women mob the Councilor and dress and equip him as a corpse.*)

600   We've got a plot. Just buy a box.
And here's a wreath for you!
A honey-cake to bribe the dog—

OLD WOMAN #1:
And holy ribbons, too—

OLD WOMAN #2:
A coin to get you on the boat—

LYSISTRATA:
605   That's all—it's time to rush off.
Charon's calling. Till he's full
He's not allowed to push off.[84]

COUNCILOR:
Such disrespect for my authority!
I'll march straight to the other councilors:
610   My person's an indictment of your deeds.

(*He exits with attendants. Lysistrata calls after him.*)

LYSISTRATA:
You're angry that we didn't lay you out?
Don't worry, sir. At dawn, two days from now,
We'll come and give you the traditional rites.

(*The women exit into the stage building.*)

MEN'S CHORUS LEADER:
Lovers of freedom, rouse yourselves from sleep!
615   Strip down, my friends, and take this problem on.

(*They remove their cloaks.*)

---

84. Grave goods reflected the myth that dead souls went to the Under-world past the guard dog Cerberus, who needed to be distracted with a cake, and over the river Styx with the boatman Charon.

CHORUS OF OLD MEN:
    I've got a whiff of larger plans at work—
    The reign of terror that we thought was gone!⁸⁵
    Suppose Laconians have gathered here   620
    With someone—oooh, with Cleisthenes, let's say⁸⁶—
    To stir this goddamn plague of women up
    And take my bare-essential jury pay.⁸⁷   625

MEN'S CHORUS LEADER:
    Scandalous! Women scold us citizens
    And blab about a war they've never seen:
    "We'll RECONCILE you with LACONIANS."
    Give me a wolf to pet—I'm just as keen.
    "I'll hide my weapon under myrtle boughs."⁸⁸   630
    This plot against our precious liberty
    I'll foil. On guard against a tyranny,
    I'll march in armor while I shop and pose
    Beside Aristogiton's statue—see!

        (Strikes a pose.)

    And here's a splendid opportunity
    To bop this impious old troll's nose!   635

        *(His fist is raised against the Women's Chorus
        Leader.)*

WOMEN'S CHORUS LEADER:
    Your mother's going to think you're someone else.
    Ladies, lay down your wraps.

        (They do so.)

CHORUS OF OLD WOMEN:
                    We're going to tell
    The city several things it needs to know.
    I owe it this. It brought me up so well: 640

---

85. The speaker refers to Hippias' tyranny, which lasted until 510 B.C.E.

86. An effeminate often made fun of in the plays of Aristophanes. The joke is on the Spartans' purported preference for anal sex.

87. The speaker's anxiety is for the pork-barrel benefits of the democracy. See note 59.

88. A line from the drinking song celebrating Harmodius and Aristogiton's plot to murder the tyrant Hippias during a festival.

At seven as a Mystery-Carrier;
A Grinder in the holy mill at ten;
645   Later, at Brauron, as a bright-robed Bear;
A comely, fig-decked Basket-Bearer then.[89]

WOMEN'S CHORUS LEADER:
That's why I'll serve my city with a chat.
So I'm a woman—why should you resent
650   That I come forward with the best advice?
I've done my share and more; it's men I've lent.
You wretched drool-bags, since the Persian Wars,
Just fritter our inheritance away,[90]
No taxes to replace the cash you spend.
655   You're going to ruin all of us someday.
You dare to gripe? Let out one vicious word,
I'll send this slipper bashing through your beard.

*(She removes a shoe and strikes a threatening
pose with it.)*

CHORUS OF OLD MEN:
Isn't this too obnoxious to ignore?
660   It started bad—how nasty can it get?
Justice and Truth rely on those with balls.

MEN'S CHORUS LEADER:
Strip off your shirts, let women smell men's sweat,
665   Stride free of wrappings hampering a fight.

(They comply.)

CHORUS OF OLD MEN:
Remember how we manned Leipsydrion?[91]

---

89. These were important ritual functions carried out by virgin girls.
The Carriers of Unspoken Things, and probably the Grinders, served
Athena; the Bears served Artemis, their terms culminating in a dance in
yellow robes at the town of Brauron. Girls carried ritual objects in bas-
kets in many processions. It was most prestigious to be selected to carry
the basket at the Panathenaea festival, the greatest celebration of Athens'
imperial glory. Fig necklaces symbolized fertility.

90. A substantial reserve fund had accumulated, starting from Persian
War spoils, but the present war had diminished it.

91. An Attic town fortified and manned briefly in the late sixth century
B.C.E. in an effort to oust the tyrant Hippias.

Shake off these rags of age and grow fresh wings!   670
Swoop like the swift young eagles we were then!

MEN'S CHORUS LEADER:
We let these wrestlers get the slightest hold,
Their grasping handiwork will never end:
They'll build themselves some ships, become marines,
Like Artemisia attacking men![92]   675
If they try horsemanship, you'd better cross
The cavalry off your list. A woman on
Her mount clings tight, however hard the ride.
She won't slip off: e.g., the Amazons
Battling in Micon's picture.[93] No, the stocks   680
Are where these girls belong, with sturdy locks!

CHORUS OF OLD WOMEN:
Give me a prod. You'll find out soon enough
My anger's like a savage, frothing boar.
You'll scream for neighbors' help: "I'm getting reamed!"   685

WOMEN'S CHORUS LEADER:
Quick, women, put your dresses on the floor.

    (They do so.)

Let the men sniff the creature so annoyed—

CHORUS OF OLD WOMEN:
If she just hears bad words, she'll bite men gory,   690
Disqualifying them for civic tasks:[94]
Cf. the beetle and the eagle story.[95]   695

WOMEN'S CHORUS LEADER:
Phooey on you! Lampito's my defense,

---

92. A queen who fought on the Persian side of the naval Battle of Salamis in 480 B.C.E.

93. Micon probably painted two famous Amazon scenes.

94. Literally, "Let someone approach me, so that he never eats garlic or black beans [again]." Soldiers ate garlic, and jurors chewed beans. See note 75.

95. In a fable, the beetle revenges herself on the eagle by rolling the bird's eggs out of the nest. Later, when eggs are held in Zeus' lap, the beetle flies up and torments the god, making him stand up and spill them.

Ismene,[96] too (a well-connected girl).
Pass seven laws against me, I don't care—
Everyone hates you, in the whole known world!
I have a friend, the sweet Boeotian eel.
I wanted her to come, the other day,

700   To share my festive rites of Hecate.[97]
Her keepers told me, "No. Because *they* say."[98]
Either you stop it or you'll learn a trick

705   You won't enjoy: to flip and break your neck.

> *(It is several days later. Enter Lysistrata, visibly distressed.)*

WOMEN'S CHORUS LEADER:
Our queenly leader, chief conspirator,
Why come you forth in such a royal snit?

LYSISTRATA:
The dastard weakness of the female mind
Bids me to pace in fury and despair.

WOMEN'S CHORUS LEADER:
710   Alas, what say you?

LYSISTRATA:
                 Naught but plainest truth.

WOMEN'S CHORUS LEADER:
What dire news? Reveal it to your friends.

LYSISTRATA:
Shameful to speak, but heavy to withhold.

WOMEN'S CHORUS LEADER:
Hide not from me our sore calamity.[99]

LYSISTRATA:
715   Well, in a word, our movement's getting fucked.

---

96. Probably the Boeotian Woman in the first scene.

97. A goddess of the Underworld.

98. See line 36 and note.

99. The preceding lines spoof the scenes in tragedy in which the chorus question a character emerging outdoors about events indoors. One line is said to come from a lost play of Euripides.

WOMEN'S CHORUS LEADER:
  Zeus!

LYSISTRATA:
  Why call on Zeus? Our nature's not *his* fault.
  And anyway, it's me who can't enforce
  Husband aversion. AWOL's spreading fast.
  The other day I caught one near Pan's cave,   720
  Making the hole a tunnel just her size.[100]
  A second sought civilian status by
  Rappelling from a crane;[101] another tried
  To ride a sparrow down to You-Know-Who's.[102]
  I had to grab her hair and drag her back.   725
  Trying for furloughs, they evoke a vast
  Supply of fiction. Here's a sample now.

      (Stops Woman #1, who has entered from the stage
      building and is dashing off toward the side.)

  Where are *you* running to?

WOMAN #1:
                              I'm going home.
  I have to rescue my—Milesian wool
  From—moths. They're going to shred it.

LYSISTRATA:
                                        Moths, my ass!   730
  Get back inside!

WOMAN #1:
                  By the Two Gods,[103] I will.
  I only need to spread it on the bed.

LYSISTRATA:
  You'll do no spreading, 'cause you're staying put.

WOMAN #1:
  I sacrifice my *wool?*

---

100. There was apparently an old hole here, narrowed or stopped up.

101. Equipment from the construction going on at the time.

102. "Orsilochus' place." He was a well-known brothel keeper. The
sparrow is Aphrodite's sacred bird.

103. Demeter and Kore.

LYSISTRATA:
>Yes, for the cause.

>*(Woman #2 enters in a tragic pose, scurrying away at
the same time.)*

WOMAN #2:
735   Pity me and my fine Amorgos flax,
       At home, left on the stems!

LYSISTRATA:
>Example B
Is skulking off to peel a pile of thread.
You, turn around!

WOMAN #2: *(Stopping reluctantly.)*
>I swear by Hecate,
I'll only stay to give it one good—shuck.

LYSISTRATA:
740   No shucking way.[104] If I give in to you,
       There's going to be no end of applicants.

>*(Woman #3 enters, clutching a protruding stomach.)*

WOMAN #3:
       Goddess of Childbirth,[105] spare me for an hour!
       This place is sacrosanct—I've got to leave![106]

LYSISTRATA:
       What *is* this crap?

WOMAN #3:
>My baby's almost here!

LYSISTRATA:
       Yesterday you weren't pregnant.

WOMAN #3:
745   >Now I am!

---

104. The untranslatable joke is that flax had to be separated from its
woody fibers, an action somewhat like pushing back the foreskin of an
uncircumcised penis before sex. The same verb is used.
105. "Eileithyia."
106. To give birth on sacred ground was not permitted.

Please, Lysistrata, let me go. The nurse
Is waiting for me.

LYSISTRATA:

Sounds a lot like bull.

(She feels the front of the woman's dress.)

There's something hard here.

WOMAN #3:

It's a baby boy.

LYSISTRATA:

By Aphrodite, not my guess at all.
It's hollow metal. Let me take a peek.   750

*(She dives under the woman's dress, emerges with a
giant helmet.)*

You idiot, the holy helmet's here![107]
You're pregnant, huh?

WOMAN #3:

By Zeus, I swear I am.

LYSISTRATA:
And what's this for?

WOMAN #3:

If I were overcome
On the way home, I'd have a kind of nest.
It seems to work for doves, at any rate.   755

LYSISTRATA:
No kidding. If that's your excuse, then wait
Five days to have a party for this hat.[108]

WOMAN #3:
But I can't even sleep here since I saw
The sacred snake.[109] You gotta let me go!

---

107. Probably from Athena's statue in the Parthenon.

108. The event named is the *amphidromia*, or family welcoming, performed five (or perhaps seven) days after the birth of a child.

109. Believed to live in a rocky crevice and associated with Erechtheus, a
mythical king of Athens. On the site, the Erechtheum, a temple to Athena, Erechtheus, and other deities, was completed in 407 B.C.E.

WOMAN #1:

760   I won't survive, I've been awake so long.
     These stupid honking owls[110] won't take a rest.

LYSISTRATA:

     Magical stuff—shut up about it, hey?
     You want your men. You don't think they want you?
     They're spending nasty nights outside your beds.
765   Dear ladies, just be patient for a bit,
     And see our project through, clear to the end.
     An oracle assures us that we'll win
     If we're united. Here, I've got the text.

WOMAN #3:

     What does it say?

LYSISTRATA:

                 Be quiet and I'll read.

(She takes out a scroll.)

770   Swallows will come together, huddling close—
     Fleeing hoopoes—renouncing phalluses[111]—
     Bad things will end, when Zeus the Thunderer
     Brings low the lofty—

WOMAN #3:

                 Hmm, we'll be on top?

LYSISTRATA:

     But if the bickering birds fly separate ways,
775   Leaving the sacred temple, it will show
     That—swallows are the world's most shameless trash.

WOMAN #3:

     The sacred words are plain. Oh, help us, gods.[112]

---

110. Associated with Athena.

111. An untranslatable pun on the word "coot."

112. Lysistrata's ploy reflects skepticism about oracles among Greek intellectuals like Aristophanes. Clients (like this group of women) could not see the genesis of an oracle within the special shrine. They had to accept whatever was brought out to them. Moreover, no such shrine was on the Acropolis; where does Lysistrata get her text? These women are

LYSISTRATA:
> We won't give in to hassles, but persist.
> Let's go inside. It would be a disgrace
> To prove unworthy of the oracle. 780

(The women exit into the stage building.)

CHORUS OF OLD MEN:
> When I was a boy, I heard a tale
> I'd like to share with you.
> There was a young man named Melanion. 785
> They told him to get married, and he said, "Pooh!"
> He fled to the mountains, where he lived,
> Hunting hares.
> He had a great dog,
> And he wove his own snares. 790
> He never went home. His hatred
> Continued burning bright.[113]
> And we hate women just as much,
> Because we know what's right. 795

MEN'S CHORUS LEADER:
> Give me a kiss, you hag.

WOMEN'S CHORUS LEADER:
> Oh, yuck, that onion smell![114]

MEN'S CHORUS LEADER:
> And now a hearty kick!

(Crotch shows as he lifts leg.)

WOMEN'S CHORUS LEADER:
> Chain up your animal! 800

---

gullible indeed. The allusion is to the myth of Philomela and Tereus, who were said to have been transformed into a swallow and a hoopoe after a particularly bad episode of domestic abuse and revenge.

113. Melanion is perhaps a deliberately odd choice as an archetypal misogynist. Elsewhere the myth stresses that he went to the wilderness to be near his beloved, the huntress Atalanta.

114. A line of uncertain meaning. However, the mention of an onion in connection with a kiss seems to point toward an interpretation like mine.

MEN'S CHORUS LEADER:
> Myronides and Phormion[115] were formidably furred:
> Their enemies took one look at them and ran.
> A nest of black hair in the crack at the back
> Is the sign of a genuine man.

CHORUS OF OLD WOMEN:
805 > It's our turn to tell you a tale.
> (We don't like the Melanion one.)
810 > Timon once lurked in the thorns,
> A wild man, the Ghouls' foster son.[116]
> He stayed away
> Till his dying day,
815 > Cursing mankind with venom.
> He loathed all of you,
> The same as we do,
820 > But was always a sweetie to women.[117]

WOMEN'S CHORUS LEADER:
> Shall I bash your jaw?

MEN'S CHORUS LEADER:
> I'll be so sore!

WOMEN'S CHORUS LEADER:
> A kick at least.

(Her leg is lifted, threatening a view of crotch.)

MEN'S CHORUS LEADER:
> Talk about beasts!

WOMEN'S CHORUS LEADER:
825 > Fine, but I'm glad that mine
> Doesn't run wild and free.
> Though I'm not especially young,
> I groom it tenderly.[118]

---

115. Two Athenian war heroes.

116. "A piece broken off the Furies," hideous, vengeful goddesses of the Underworld.

117. Timon was a fifth-century B.C.E. Athenian legendary for misanthropy but not misandry. This example is almost as distorted as that of Melanion.

118. See line 89 and note.

(The choruses step back.)

(Lysistrata appears on the roof of the stage building.)

LYSISTRATA:
Whoopee! Get over here, you women, quick!

(Enter Woman #1, Myrrhine, and several other women onto the roof.)

WOMAN #1:
What is it? Tell me what you're squalling at. 830

LYSISTRATA:
A man—he's coming in a frenzied charge,
With Aphrodite's offering—of meat.
O Queen of Cyprus and of Cythera
And Paphos! (Yeah, bud, come *straight up* to us!)

WOMAN #1:
Where is our mystery man?

LYSISTRATA:
By Chloe's shrine.[119] 835

WOMAN #1:
No question—that thing's male. Who could he be?

LYSISTRATA:
All of you look. Does someone know him?

MYRRHINE:
Zeus!
I do. My husband—it's Cinesias.[120]

LYSISTRATA:
Your duty is to roast him on that spit.
You will, you won't, you might—just lead him on. 840
Remember, though: you swore on booze—no sex!

MYRRHINE:
Leave it to me.

---

119. A spot sacred to Demeter Chloe ("Demeter of Greenery").
120. From the Greek word for "fuck."

LYSISTRATA:
>   But I'll stay here and pull
> The opening stunts and get him all worked up
> For you to play with. Go back in and hide.

> *(All the women but Lysistrata exit. Enter Cinesias,*
> *with his Slave, who is carrying Cinesias' Baby. A*
> *giant codpiece hangs from Cinesias' waist. Lysistrata*
> *descends by ladder or through the stage building to*
> *meet Cinesias.)*

CINESIAS:
845   I'm screwed—I mean I'm not! I'm stretched so tight
      Skilled torture couldn't do a better job.

LYSISTRATA:
Who's gotten past the sentinels?

CINESIAS:
>   It's me.

LYSISTRATA:
A man?

CINESIAS:
>   Yeah, can't you see?

LYSISTRATA:
>   I see. Get lost.

CINESIAS:
Who's going to throw me out?

LYSISTRATA:
>   The lookout. Me.

CINESIAS:
850   I need Myrrhine. Call her for me—please.

LYSISTRATA:
Myrrhine? Huh? You need her? Who are you?

CINESIAS:
Her husband. I'm Cinesias from—[121]

---

121. The Greek text includes the deme name, which is a double-entendre
in line with Cinesias' name. See previous note.

LYSISTRATA:

Hey!
I know *you*, or I've often heard your name.
All of us know it. You're quite famous here.
Your wife's mouth never takes a break from you.   855
She toasts you every time she has a snack—
Smooth eggs, or juicy apples—

CINESIAS:

Gods! O gods!

LYSISTRATA:

Just Aphrodite. When we mention men,
That wife of yours declares without delay:
"They're all a pile of crud compared to mine."   860

CINESIAS:
Call her, c'mon.

LYSISTRATA:

And what's it worth to you?

CINESIAS:
What have I got on me? Oh, right, there's *this*.
It's all I have, but you can take it and—

LYSISTRATA:
There, now. I'll call her down to you.

CINESIAS:

And fast.

(Lysistrata exits into stage building.)

There's nothing now in life to bring me joy.   865
She left the house! She left me on my own!
When I return at night, the whole place seems
So empty, and I ache. The food has got
No taste for me. All I can feel is dick.

*(Myrrhine appears on the roof of the stage building,
calling behind her.)*

MYRRHINE:
I love him, oh, I do! He won't accept   870
My yearning love. Don't make me go out there.

CINESIAS:
   Myrrhine, I don't get it, baby doll.
   Come down here.

MYRRHINE:
                         That event will not occur.

CINESIAS:
   I call, Myrrhine, and you won't come down?

MYRRHINE:
875   What the hell for? Why are you bothering?

CINESIAS:
   What *for?* To keep my prick from crushing me.

MYRRHINE:
   See you around.

CINESIAS:
                    No—listen to your son.
   (To Baby.) You little—call your Mama, or I'll—

BABY:
                                        Waaah!
   Mama! Mama! Mama!

CINESIAS:
880   What's wrong with you? No feeling for your child?
   Six days he's gone without a bath or food.

MYRRHINE:
   Poor baby. Daddy doesn't give a hoot.

CINESIAS:
   Monster, at least come down and feed your whelp.

MYRRHINE:
   Ah, motherhood! What choice do I have now?

      (She descends and approaches him.)

CINESIAS: *(Aside.)*
885   Maybe my mind's just soggy, but she seems
   Wonderfully young—her face has such allure.
   And see that snippy way she struts along.
   It's making me so horny I could croak.

MYRRHINE: *(Taking Baby.)*
 My lovey-pie—too bad about your Dad.
 Give Mommy kiss, my honey-dumpling-bun.   890

CINESIAS:
 What are you up to here? What have they done
 To lure you off? Why are you hurting me?
 You're hurting too!

   (He reaches for her.)

MYRRHINE:
                    Your hand can stop right there.

CINESIAS:
 My stuff at home—it's your stuff too—is shot
 Since you've been gone.

MYRRHINE:
                    My, my, that's too, *too* bad.   895

CINESIAS:
 That nicest cloth of yours—the hens got in—
 You ought to see it.

MYRRHINE:
                    Only if I cared.

CINESIAS:
 And all this time we've ditched the rituals
 Of Aphrodite. Aren't you coming back?

MYRRHINE:
 Not me, by Zeus, unless you make a deal   900
 To stop this war.

CINESIAS:
                    If that's the way we vote,
 That's what we'll do.

MYRRHINE:
                    Then you trot off and vote,
 And I'll trot home. For now, I've sworn to stay.

CINESIAS:
 Then lie down here with me. It's been so long.

MYRRHINE:
905   No, not a chance—in spite of how I feel.

CINESIAS:
    You love me? Honey, then why not lie down?

MYRRHINE:
    Don't be ridiculous! The baby's here.

CINESIAS:
    Right. Yeah. Okay. Boy, you can take it home.

    (Slave takes Baby back and exits.)

    There, do you see a baby anymore?
    So if you'd just—

MYRRHINE:
910   You're crazy! Where's a spot
    To do it here?

CINESIAS:
                    Uh, there's the grove of Pan.

MYRRHINE:
    And how am I to purify myself?

CINESIAS:
    No sweat. There's the Clepsydra you can use.[122]

MYRRHINE:
    I swore an *oath*. And now I break my word?

CINESIAS:
915   Forget your oath. 'Cause that's my lookout, huh?

MYRRHINE:
    I'll get a cot for us.

CINESIAS:
                    No, stay right here.
    The ground is fine.

MYRRHINE:
                    Apollo help me, no!
    Stretch till you twang, before I lay you there!

---

122. A spring. She could not return to the sacred ground of the Acropolis without bathing.

(She exits.)

CINESIAS:
There's no mistaking such a doting fuss.

(She returns with a cot.)

MYRRHINE:
Hurry, lie down. I'm going to get undressed. 920

(Cinesias lies down.)

Now what—? I've got to drag a mattress out.

CINESIAS:
But I don't care!

MYRRHINE:
By Artemis, you can't
Think we could do it on the cords.

CINESIAS:
Kiss me.

MYRRHINE:
Okay.

(She kisses him.)

CINESIAS:
Fantastic. You come back real fast.

(She exits, returns with a mattress, nudges Cinesias off the cot, and places the mattress on it.)

MYRRHINE:
Mattress. All right. Lie down.

(She rearranges him.)

I'll soon be nude! 925
Whoops! I forgot—something—a pillow, yes!

CINESIAS:
But I don't need one.

MYRRHINE:
That's too bad. I do.

(She exits.)

CINESIAS:
Oh, what an epic prank on my poor prick![123]

(She returns with a pillow.)

MYRRHINE:
Head up. *(She places the pillow under his head.)* I've got the
whole collection now.

CINESIAS:
930   I'm sure you do. Come here, my cutie-sweet.

MYRRHINE:
Just let me get this bra off. One more time:
You wouldn't lead me on about the peace?

CINESIAS:
If I do that, Zeus strike me dead.

MYRRHINE:
                         A sheet!

CINESIAS:
By Zeus, forget the sheet! I want to screw!

MYRRHINE:
935   Don't worry, you'll get screwed. I'll be right back.

(She exits.)

CINESIAS:
She's going to decorate until I die.

(She enters with a sheet.)

MYRRHINE:
Up just a little. *(She spreads the sheet under him.)*

CINESIAS:
                    (Indicating penis.) How is *this* for up?

MYRRHINE:
Do you want oil?

---

123. "This penis is being entertained [like] Heracles." A common motif
in comedy was the teasing and cheating of this greedy, lustful god.

CINESIAS:

No! By Apollo! No!

MYRRHINE:

My, looks like you don't know what's good for you.

(She exits.)

CINESIAS:

Great Zeus in heaven, make the bottle spill!   940

(She returns with oil bottle.)

MYRRHINE:

Hold out your hand, take some, and spread it on.

(He takes a sample.)

CINESIAS:

Yuck, I don't like it. All I smell's delay.
It's got no nuance of MY WIFE and SEX.

MYRRHINE:

Well, shame on me! I brought the one from Rhodes.

CINESIAS:

No, never mind, it's perfect.

MYRRHINE:

You're a dork.   945

(She exits.)

CINESIAS:

Perfume's inventor ought to cram the stuff.

(She enters, offers him a bottle.)

MYRRHINE:

Take this.

CINESIAS:

I've *got* one that's about to crack![124]
Lie down, you tramp! Don't bring me anything!

---

124. Oil bottles, about the size and shape of an erect penis, made for
good sight gags.

MYRRHINE:
Okay, I'm lying down.

(*She perches on edge of bed.*)

I've only got
950 To get my shoes off. Honey, don't forget:
You're voting for a treaty.

CINESIAS:

I'll assess—

(*She dashes away and exits.*)

Shit! Shit!! She's gone. She rubbed me out and ran.
She plucked my cock,[125] consigning me to dust.

Oh, woe! Whom shall I screw?[126]
955 The loveliest one is gone.
Who'll take this orphan on?
I need a pimp! Hey, you—[127]
Go hire me a nanny for my dong.

CHORUS OF OLD MEN:
Misery, woe on woe!
Lo, I brim over with compassion:
960 You're foully swindled of your ration!
Forsooth, your guts are going to blow!
How will your nuts remain
Intact? Will you not go insane?
965 Your manly parts are out of luck
Without their regular morning fuck.

CINESIAS:
Great Zeus, how dreadfully I twitch!

CHORUS OF OLD MEN:
That's from the world's most evil bitch.

---

125. The image is of the foreskin pulled back in agonized readiness for
sex. See lines 735–40 and note, and line 1136.

126. The following exchange is a parody of the exchange with the chorus at the crisis of a tragedy.

127. In the Greek text, Cinesias summons "Dog-Fox," the nickname of
the procurer Philostratus; many of Aristophanes' comic victims would
have been sitting in the theater, so actors may be imagined addressing
them directly.

She tortured you, the filthy cheat.

CHORUS OF OLD WOMEN:
No, no! She's absolutely sweet.   970

CHORUS OF OLD MEN:
She's a curse. She's a disease.

CINESIAS:
She is! O Zeus, please, please!
You know the way your whirlwind flips
And flings the brush piles that it whips?
And twists and loops them in a blur,   975
And dumps them down? Do that to her.
But when you let her touch the ground
She must land tidily around
My prong, okay? And right away?

(*Enter Spartan Herald, bent over and holding his
cloak out in front. Cinesias has recovered enough of
his composure to face him.*)

SPARTAN HERALD:
Where do you find the Elders in this town?   980
No, sorry, your—Directors?[128] I got news.

CINESIAS:
Are you a human being or a pole?[129]

SPARTAN HERALD:
By the Twin Gods,[130] I've come official-like
From Sparta, 'cause we need to compromise.

CINESIAS:
Then please explain that pike beneath your clothes.   985

---

128. Sparta was governed differently, and Spartans were notoriously parochial. This herald names the Council of Elders (Spartan) and then the *prytaneis* (Athenian, translated here as "Directors"). The Athenian administrative year was divided into ten parts, during each of which fifty different members—the Prytany Council—of the Council of Five Hundred presided.

129. "Conisalus," a fertility spirit represented with a giant phallus.

130. Castor and Polydeuces.

SPARTAN HERALD: *(Dodging Cinesias' eyes.)*
  I swear, it's nothing.

CINESIAS:
                          But you're turned away.
  Your cloak is hiding something. Have you got
  Some swelling from the ride?

SPARTAN HERALD: *(Aside.)*
                          His mind is gone.

CINESIAS:
  Come on, you scamming bastard, it's a bone!

SPARTAN HERALD:
990   By Zeus, it ain't. Back off, you crazy fart.

CINESIAS:
  What is it, then?

SPARTAN HERALD:
                          Uh, it's a Spartan staff.[131]

CINESIAS: *(Opening cloak.)*
  Then here's a Spartan staff that's just changed sides.
  I know the whole thing. You can tell the truth
  About what Lacedaemon's going through.

SPARTAN HERALD:
995   Well, us and our confederate states is stuck.
  Stuck standing up. We need to *snatch* a piece.[132]

CINESIAS:
  And who's the source of this catastrophe?
  Pan?[133]

---

131. These staffs were an early coding device. One remained in Sparta, and a Spartan diplomat abroad carried one of the exact same size and shape. A message was written on a strip wound around one staff and had to be wound around the duplicate staff to be deciphered.

132. "We need Pellene." The name plays on those of a prostitute and of a territory Sparta coveted.

133. The god Pan (the origin of our word "panic") was thought to induce various kinds of mass afflictions.

SPARTAN HERALD:
    No, Lampito—I think it was her plan.
    And then all over Sparta, when they heard,
    The women thundered from the starting line—   1000
    There went our pussy in a cloud of dust.

CINESIAS:
    How are you making out, then?

SPARTAN HERALD:
                       Hey, we're *not*.
    The whole damn town's bent double like we's kicked.[134]
    Before we lay a finger on a twat,
    The women say we gotta all wise up   1005
    And make a treaty with the other Greeks.

CINESIAS:
    They got together and they plotted this,
    All of the women. I can see it now.
    Quick, have the Spartans send ambassadors,
    Fully empowered to reach a settlement.   1010
    And on the evidence of this my dick
    I'll make our Council choose some legates too.

SPARTAN HERALD:
    I'm off. You got the whole thing figured out.

       (They exit.)

MEN'S CHORUS LEADER:
    To get on top of women—try a fire,
    It's easier. A leopard's got more shame.   1015

WOMEN'S CHORUS LEADER:
    And knowing this, you won't give up this fight,
    When you can always trust me as a friend?

MEN'S CHORUS LEADER:
    Women revolt me. And it stays that way.

WOMEN'S CHORUS LEADER:
    There's lots of time. But I can't bear to see

---

134. The image in the Greek is of men bent over, protecting lighted lamps
from the wind.

1020   You standing garmentless. You look absurd.
        I'll come and put this cloak back over you.

        (She drapes it around him.)

MEN'S CHORUS LEADER:
        By Zeus, you've done a thing that isn't vile.
        I stripped when I was raging for a fight.

WOMEN'S CHORUS LEADER:
        Now you're a man again, and not a clown.
1025   If you were nice, I might have grabbed that beast
        Still lodging in your eye, and plucked him out.

MEN'S CHORUS LEADER:
        So that's what's galling me. Here, take my ring.
        Gouge out the critter, let me see him. Gods,
        All day he's masticated in that lair.

WOMEN'S CHORUS LEADER:
1030   For sure, here goes. But what a grouchy guy.

        (Removes bug.)

        Oh, Zeus, I've never seen a gnat this big.
        Just look. It's like some monster from the swamp.[135]

MEN'S CHORUS LEADER:
        You helped. That thing was excavating me . . .
        And now it's gone. There's water in my eyes.

WOMEN'S CHORUS LEADER:
1035   I'll wipe it off, though you've been quite a pain.

        (She wipes his face and kisses him.)

        And here's a kiss.

MEN'S CHORUS LEADER:
                            No—

WOMEN'S CHORUS LEADER:
                                It's not up to you!

MEN'S CHORUS LEADER:
        Up your wazoo! You're born to flatter us!

---

135. Tricorythus is the swampy area named.

The adage says it all: that women are
Abomination indispensable.
But let's make peace, and in the time to come　　　　1040
I'll neither dump on you nor take your crap.
Let's all line up and dance to celebrate.

> *(The two choruses unite and address the*
> *audience.)*

UNITED CHORUS:
Gentlemen, I don't mean to call
A fellow citizen a snot or blot
Or anything like that at all.　　　　　　　　　　1045
No, *au contraire!* I'll be much more than fair!
Sufficient are the evils that you've got.[136]
Man or woman, just tell me
If you'd like a bit—　　　　　　　　　　　　　1050
Two thousand, or, say, three—[137]
I've got so much of it.
We'll even give you bags to haul it.
In peaceful times we won't recall it:　　　　　　1055
Just keep the goodies from our coffers.
Oops: we've forgotten what we offered.

We've just invited really swell
Carystians, from overseas.[138]
We're going to entertain them well,　　　　　　1060
With perfectly braised, tenderly glazed
Piglet served with purée of peas.
Spruce yourself up (don't leave out
The kids!) and come today.　　　　　　　　　　1065
March in, nothing to ask about,
And no one in the way.
Barge boldly to the doors.
Pretend the place is yours.
Don't even bother to knock—　　　　　　　　　1070
It's going to be locked.

---

136. Abuse of the audience was a long-standing comic tradition.
137. "Two or three minas," the equivalent of several thousand dollars.
138. See line 1181 and note.

*(The Spartan Ambassadors approach, bent over, hold-
ing their cloaks out in front, trying to conceal massive
erections. Slaves accompany them.)*

UNITED CHORUS LEADER:
  Here come the Spartan legates, beards a-drag—
  In clothing that looks draped around a crate.
  Laconian gentlemen, our best to you!
1075   Tell us in what condition you've arrived.

SPARTAN AMBASSADOR:
  This isn't gonna take a wordy talk.

      (Opens cloak.)

  A look-see for yourselves should do the trick.

UNITED CHORUS LEADER:
  Oh, wow. The situation's pretty tense,
  A crisis getting more and more inflamed.

SPARTAN AMBASSADOR:
1080   It's crazy. Anyway, what's there to say?
  We'll accept any kind of terms for peace.

      *(Enter Athenian Ambassadors, like the Spartans
      under obvious strain. Slaves accompany them also.)*

UNITED CHORUS LEADER:
  These natives have a tic a lot like yours,
  Of bending down like wrestlers, with a lot
  Of room for something underneath their cloaks.
1085   They have some hypertrophy of the groin.

ATHENIAN AMBASSADOR #1: *(To United Chorus.)*
  Where's Lysistrata? Someone's got to know.

      *(Pulls cloak aside to display contents, gestures toward
      Spartans.)*

  We're here, they're here, but both are way up there.

UNITED CHORUS LEADER:
  I seem to see a certain parallel
  Between these two diseases—cramps at dawn?

ATHENIAN AMBASSADOR #1:
    Worse, we've arrived at wits' and gonads' end.   1090
    If we don't hurry and negotiate,
    We'll have to make a date with Cleisthenes.[139]

UNITED CHORUS LEADER:
    If I were you, I'd cover up those things.
    What if a prankster with a chisel sees?[140]

ATHENIAN AMBASSADOR #1:
    That's good advice.

    (Covers himself.)

SPARTAN AMBASSADOR:
                By the Twin Gods, it is.   1095
    We better wrap these bigger duds around.

    (Covers himself likewise.)

ATHENIAN AMBASSADOR #1:
    Greetings to you, dear Spartans. We've been stiffed.

SPARTAN AMBASSADOR:
    And us, too, pal. Maybe the audience
    Could see that we was playing with ourselves.

ATHENIAN AMBASSADOR #1:
    Let's get through our agenda double-quick.   1100
    What do you want?

SPARTAN AMBASSADOR:
                We're the ambassadors.
    We're here about a treaty.

ATHENIAN AMBASSADOR #1:
                So are we.
    But only Lysistrata's up to it.
    Let's ask her. She can be the referee.

---

139. See line 621 and note.

140. The chorus warn about the "Herm-cutters," whoever cut the penises off the Hermae, or guardian statues in front of houses, before the Sicilian expedition starting in 415 B.C.E. The disastrous outcome of the expedition was thought to owe something to the bad omen.

SPARTAN AMBASSADOR:
1105   Lysis or Strata—anyone who can.[141]

> *(Enter Lysistrata.)*

ATHENIAN AMBASSADOR #1:
It looks like there's no need for us to call.
She heard us. She's already coming out.

UNITED CHORUS LEADER:
You who've got by far the biggest balls of all,
Show you've got the greatest tact and gall of all!
Be high-class, low-class, sweet, self-righteous—everything.
1110   Every last minister in Greece now stumbles
Under your spell, surrendering his grumbles.

LYSISTRATA:
It's not hard work. You only have to swoop
The moment when they're bursting for a deal.
But here's the test. Goddess of Deals, come out!

> *(Reconciliation, an actor in a body stocking padded to
> look like a nude woman, enters.)*

1115   To start with, take the Spartans by the hand—
And don't get rough, don't have it all your way;
Don't wreck it like our stupid husbands did.
Be gentle as a mother in her house—
But if he pulls his hand back, take his dong.
1120   Lead the Athenians to center stage.
(Anything you can grab can be the leash.)
Laconian gentlemen, stand close to me,
And our guys here, and hear my reasons out.

> *(Reconciliation has arranged the Athenian and
> Spartan Ambassadors on either side of Lysistrata.)*

I am a woman, but I have a mind
1125   That wasn't bad to start with, and I got
A first-class education listening

---

141. A joke on the name Lysistrata (see note 1): "Also Lysistratus [a male
Lysistrata; there was an Athenian of this name, whom the comic play-
wrights mock] if you want." In either case, the name means that peace
will be made.

To Father and the elders year on year.
I now shall do what's right and give you hell
Together, for a single holy bowl
Sprinkles fraternal altars at the games: 1130
Delphic, Pylaean, and Olympian.[142]
I could go on and on and on and on!
You see barbarian armies threatening,[143]
But you destroy the towns and lives of Greeks.
That's quite a climax to my preface, huh?   1135

ATHENIAN AMBASSADOR #1:
   What? This bald behemoth is killing me.[144]

LYSISTRATA:
   Laconians, I'm turning now to you.
   Don't you remember how a suppliant
   From Sparta, Pericleidas, roosted here,
   Next to the altar,[145] pale (his uniform   1140
   Bright red), and begged for troops. Messene and
   Poseidon both at once had shaken you.
   And Cimon took four thousand armored men
   And made your territory safe again.[146]
   After this gift from the Athenians,   1145
   You come and rip their land apart as thanks?

ATHENIAN AMBASSADOR #1:
   Right, Lysistrata! Bunch of criminals!

   *(Spartan Ambassador is enthralled by
   Reconciliation.)*

---

142. A number of international festival competitions helped the Hellenic world in its self-definition. The Olympics were held at Pisa, the Pylaea at Thermopylae, and the Pythia at Delphi.

143. The Persian empire hovered continually, looking for advantages.

144. See lines 735–40 and note, and line 953.

145. A suppliant gave his request religious meaning by putting himself under the gods' protection while making it.

146. This seems an odd choice of example. After an earthquake (Poseidon was thought to cause earthquakes) and the revolt of the Messenian helots (or serfs) in 464 B.C.E., the general Cimon did go to Sparta, but the Spartans were suspicious and sent him home before he had a chance to help. The episode caused much bad feeling between the two states.

SPARTAN AMBASSADOR:
I guess we are—that's such a gorgeous ass.[147]

LYSISTRATA:
You think I'm going to spare my countrymen?

(*Turns to Athenians.*)

1150   Laconians once came to rescue you—
You only had the sheepskins on your backs.
The Spartans, marching out with you one day,
Erased large numbers of Thessalian goons.
A single ally made you Hippias-free:
1155   Denuded of the rags of refugees,
And draped in your own polity again.[148]

SPARTAN AMBASSADOR: (*Staring at Reconciliation.*)
I never seen a woman so first-rate.

ATHENIAN AMBASSADOR #1: (*Staring likewise.*)
I've never gazed on such a spiffy quim.

LYSISTRATA:
With these good deeds already on the tab,
1160   Why squabble like a bunch of stupid jerks?
Be reconciled. There's nothing in the way.

(*In the following scene, Reconciliation serves
as a map.*)

SPARTAN AMBASSADOR:
Okay, if we can have this little loop,
We're in.

ATHENIAN AMBASSADOR #1:
What's that, my friend?

SPARTAN AMBASSADOR:
Pylos, I mean.
For years we've tried to get a finger in.[149]

---

147. Literally, "rectum," the notorious Spartan preference.

148. The Spartans helped exiled Athenian clans to overthrow the tyranny of Hippias (with his Thessalian cavalry bodyguards) in 510 B.C.E.

149. It was of great strategic importance that the Athenians had controlled the fortified city of Pylos, on the western coast of the Peloponnese,

ATHENIAN AMBASSADOR #1:
  Poseidon help me, *that* you will not do. 1165

LYSISTRATA:
  Let go.

ATHENIAN AMBASSADOR #1:
      But I've got uprisings to quell!

LYSISTRATA:
  Just ask them for another piece instead.

ATHENIAN AMBASSADOR #1:
  Give me this thingy—this cute brushy bit,
  And this deep gulf behind, which I'll explore—
  And these nice legs of land: I want them too.[150] 1170

SPARTAN AMBASSADOR:
  Buddy, you can't have every friggin' thing!

LYSISTRATA:
  Hey! Make some compromise and part the legs.

ATHENIAN AMBASSADOR #1:
  I'm going to strip right down and start to plow.

SPARTAN AMBASSADOR:
  I'm going to spread manure on my field.[151]

LYSISTRATA:
  And you can do it when you're reconciled. 1175
  If you're quite ready for a settlement,
  Then scatter and confer with your allies.

ATHENIAN AMBASSADOR #1:
  Why bother? Situated in my prong,

---

since 425 B.C.E. The lines include a pun on "anus," another reference to the Spartans' alleged predilection.

150. A series of geographical puns. The name of the Spartan ally Echinous sounds like the Greek for "sea urchin" or "hedgehog," indicating pubic hair. Echinous is here mentioned as on the Malian Gulf, "gulf" probably meaning the vagina. The "Megarian legs" were strategic walls.

151. The poet Hesiod orders farmers to plow, sow, and reap "naked," i.e., without their outer garments. Again, Aristophanes jokes about Spartans and anal sex.

They'll judge precisely as I do. They'll want
To screw—

SPARTAN AMBASSADOR:

1180 　　　　　　　And ours are just like yours, I swear—

ATHENIAN AMBASSADOR #1:
And our Carystians especially.[152]

LYSISTRATA:
You're both correct! While you're still abstinent,
We'll have the women on the citadel
Open their boxes for you.[153] You can feast
1185 And then exchange your pledges of good faith.
Then each of you can take his wife and go
Straight home—

ATHENIAN AMBASSADOR #1:
　　　　　　　Finally. Let's not stand around.

SPARTAN AMBASSADOR:
Show me—

ATHENIAN AMBASSADOR #1:
　　　　　　The fastest exit we can make.

*(Lysistrata and the Ambassadors exit together,
leaving the slaves, who settle down outside the
stage building.)*

UNITED CHORUS:
Embroidered throws to beat the cold,
1190 Dresses and capes—none better, a
Big pile of jewelry, solid gold—
Send kids to take the stuff away,
For Basket-Bearing girls,[154] et cetera.
1195 "Help yourselves," I always say,
"To anything you find.

---

152. Several sexual puns are possible on the name of these important allies of Athens.

153. See lines 912–3 and note; men as well as women were forbidden to enter a holy place immediately after sex. The ironic double-entendre on "boxes" is original in the Greek.

154. See line 646 and note.

I don't seal up the jars or check
What money's left behind."[155]   1200
In fact, there's nothing left at all,
Unless I'm going blind.

Not enough bread,
But slaves to feed,
And hosts of hungry kids?
I've got plenty of baby-fine wheat   1205
For every citizen in need.
This dust grows into strapping loaves to eat.
Come in—bring duffel bags and sacks!   1210
My slave will stuff them full with any
Dry goods that you lack.
Too bad my dog will fuck you up.
He's waiting at the back.   1215

> *(Slaves sprawl sleepily in front of stage building.*
> *Thick-voiced Athenian Ambassador #1 pounds on the*
> *door from inside.)*

ATHENIAN AMBASSADOR #1:
Open!

> *(Barges through, knocking slave in front of door out of*
> *the way. Ambassador is garlanded, unsteady on his*
> *feet, and carrying a torch.)*

That's what you get for bein' there!

> *(Begins kicking and pushing dazed slaves.)*

And you guys too—what if I take this torch
And carbonize you? *(To audience.)* What a dumb cliché.[156]
I'm not going through with it. Okay! Calm down!
To make you happy I can play a boob.   1220

> *(Athenian Ambassador #2, similar in appearance,*
> *enters from same door.)*

ATHENIAN AMBASSADOR #2:
I'll help. Two boobs beat one—like this one here.

---

155. Coins were stored in sealed jars.

156. The slapstick of beating slaves and chasing them with torches was
overused in Old Comedy but seems to have been a crowd pleaser.

(Assaults slave.)

Haul ass! Or you'll be howling for your hair.

ATHENIAN AMBASSADOR #1:
    Throw yourselves out! Our Spartan guests inside
    Don't want to kick their way through piles of you.

    (Slaves flee.)

ATHENIAN AMBASSADOR #2:
1225   I've never seen a party good as this.
    Those Spartans sure are fun—now who'da thought?
    And we're a damn sight smarter when we're drunk.

ATHENIAN AMBASSADOR #1:
    I tell ya, being sober's bad for us.
    I'm gonna move that anyone we send
1230   Anywhere to negotiate, get sloshed.
    The trouble's been, we're sober when we go
    To Sparta, so we're spoilers from the start.
    What they *do* say, we're not prepared to hear.
    And everything they *don't* say, we assume.
1235   We've all got different versions in the end.
    But now we're fine. Someone sang "Telamon"
    When what we wanted was "Cleitagora":[157]
    We slapped him on the back and told him, "Great!"

    (Slaves slink back onstage.)

    I can't believe those slaves are comin' back.
1240   Get out! The whip is looking for you guys.

        *(Slaves exit. Spartan Ambassadors enter, with
        a Piper.)*

ATHENIAN AMBASSADOR #2:
    Already we've got Spartans walking through.

SPARTAN AMBASSADOR: *(To Piper.)*
    Hey, my best buddy, can we hear the pipes?
    There's something good I got to dance and sing.
    It's for our friends in Athens—and for us.

---

157. Traditional drinking songs based on mythology and legend.

ATHENIAN AMBASSADOR #1:
    Zeus blast us if those pipes can't use a blast.   1245
    It's wonderful to watch you Spartans dance.

      (The Piper strikes up a tune.)

SPARTAN AMBASSADOR:
    Memory, rouse, for my young sake,
    The Muse who knows of both our nations:
    How, godlike, the Athenians at Artemisium   1250
    Smashed the hulls of the Medes and were victorious,
    While Leonidas led us Spartans
    Fierce as boars sharpening their tusks;   1255
    Foam blossomed over our jaws,
    Ran down our legs.
    The Persians were as
    Many as the sand grains.[158]   1260
    Huntress in the wilderness,
    Come to us, O holy virgin,
    Bless our treaty,
    Unite us forever.   1265
    May our friendship
    Never be troubled.
    May our bond turn us
    From wily foxes into men.   1270
    Come, O come,
    Maiden with your pack of hounds.[159]

      (Enter Lysistrata with the Athenian and Spartan Women.)

ATHENIAN AMBASSADOR #1:
    All but one thing is nicely put to bed.
    Reclaim your wives,[160] Laconians, and we
    Will take our own. Each woman by her man,   1275
    And each man by his woman, celebrate,
    Give thanks in joyful dances for the gods,
    And vow to never go so wrong again.

---

158. In 480 B.C.E., the Athenians fought the Persian navy off Artemisium in Euboea, while the Spartans held the pass at Thermopylae against the Persian infantry.

159. Artemis.

160. The hostages mentioned in line 244.

*(The couples join the United Chorus, and all
dance in pairs.)*

Bring on the dancers, invite the Graces,
1280   Call Artemis and her twin, God of the joyous cry,
To lead the dance; and call the god of Nysa,
His eyes glittering, companion of the maenads;
1285   And Zeus of the lightning bolt, and his blessed consort,[161]
And all the spirits[162] as witnesses
Forever mindful of gentle Peace,
1290   Whom the goddess Cypris[163] gave us.

UNITED CHORUS:
Shout to the gods,
Leap up, rejoice.
A victory dance,
A holy song!

ATHENIAN AMBASSADOR #1:
1295   Add a new song to my new song.

SPARTAN AMBASSADOR:
Spartan Muse, come once more,
Leave your pretty Taygetus.[164]
Help us hymn in fitting words Apollo in Amyclae,[165]
1300   And Athena of the Bronze House,[166]
And the noble children of Tyndareos
Who play beside the Eurotas.[167]
Start off lightly
And jump up high.
1305   Sing for Sparta,
Where thudding feet
Worship the gods.

---

161. Apollo was Artemis' twin. Dionysus had ecstatic female worshipers, the maenads. Hera was Zeus' wife.

162. The *daimones* or minor deities.

163. Aphrodite.

164. See line 117 and note.

165. This shrine of his was outside the city of Sparta.

166. A temple in Sparta.

167. Castor and Polydeuces; Sparta's famous river.

The girls like colts
Leap by the river.
Their steps pound.   1310
The dust rises.
They frisk and shake their hair
Like bacchants with their wands.
And Leda's daughter leads them,
Lovely, holy patroness of the chorus.[168]   1315

Tie your hair back, let your footsteps fall
With the speed of a deer's, and clap your hands.
Our Goddess of the Bronze House has victory over all. 1320

(*All exit, singing and dancing.*)

---

168. Helen was worshiped as a goddess in Sparta.

Commentary 1

Athenian Democracy

Lysistrata is a play about democracy. At the beginning, the women form a mock Assembly of the people. Lysistrata, in the role of demagogue, or charismatic, unofficial leader, persuades the others to swear to a sexual boycott. The older women make war together, storming the Acropolis, and the younger ones join them in defending it. The counterattackers, the Chorus of Old Men, suspect an oligarchic coup and repeat the accusation later. The Councilor, a member of a special government board that at this time largely superseded the Council of Five Hundred, enters to sort things out. He makes a resentful speech about the Assembly that voted for the ill-thought-out Sicilian expedition. Unable to cope with the women in scuffle and argument, he stomps off to tattle to his fellow board members. The raucous exchange of factional insults continues. Lysistrata works hard to consolidate her own faction. Cinesias cannot reassure his wife as to his intention to make peace, because he regards it as a decision to be made by the mass of male citizens. Fortunately, he is wrong. Meeting the Spartan Herald, who is on a peace mission, he instructs him to fetch ambassadors and sets off to the Council of Five Hundred to get Athenian counterparts. Under Lysistrata's guidance, the negotiation is successful, and a celebratory banquet follows.

However critical of the system in other respects, this play shows the government functioning well enough to make peace when sensible people recognize the need. But the story contains sly modifications of democratic structures. If Cinesias were to stick to his plan for debating and voting about peace, a procedure that ordinarily entailed a motion from the Council but could not have left out the Assembly, any hope of a settlement would fizzle out. In the Assembly, all male citizens could participate, and the poor—with their shortsighted financial interest in war—were in the majority. In the play's alternative universe, the handling of foreign policy solely by another body saves the day.

Aristophanes' rewriting of the constitution has its historical context. The radical democracy had helped generate and aggravate the disastrous Peloponnesian War, in a brain fever lit by the

notion that the poor, just by being Athenians, could become end-
lessly better off through the wealth of empire. Aristophanes
counters by stressing the need for farsighted, sensible leadership,
cooperation, and compromise; these are for him the unradical
components of peace. Had he been in the business of recommending constitutional reforms, Aristophanes would have sug-
gested measures to reduce the power of the "lowlifes" mentioned
in 170f. He makes a persuasive case that it was at least partly
these citizens' insecure, obsessive sense of entitlement that prevented necessary dialogue. He vividly sets out their attitude
through the Chorus of Old Men.

Many of Aristophanes' contemporaries recognized the dam-
age done by radical intransigence, but by this time the government was too weak to defend itself against Persian, Spartan, and
domestic intrigue. Only a few months after the play was performed, the dictatorial Four Hundred pushed aside the constitution and popular decision making. Still in 411 B.C.E., Theramenes
brought in a moderate regime. Had it been up to him and not the
rank and file of the navy, Athens would have made a quite favorable peace with Sparta after winning the Battle of Cyzicus in 410
B.C.E. Instead, the victory led back to hawkish radical democracy,
presided over now by the demagogue Cleophon, pork-barrel dis-
tributor par excellence; and the grabby recklessness Aristophanes
despised worsened. A far-right reign of terror followed Athens'
loss of the war in 404 B.C.E. I doubt the playwright went around
saying, "If only you had listened to me . . . ," but he could have.

It is commonly thought that the Athenian democracy was the
ideological model for participatory government in the modern
world. God forbid. With a few exceptions, the American democratic experiment has been stodgy and cautious from its beginning. Most Americans prize its negative quality, the slowness of
the government to do things to them or to prevent them from
doing things.

Athenian democracy was far different, and one of the most
important measures of this was the weight of esteem and expectation it bore. Accountable government was a recent, impressive
invention. Draco had introduced written law to the city only in
the late seventh century B.C.E. All over the Greek world, through
Aristophanes' time and beyond, the horrors of the Dark Ages
(about 1100 to 800 B.C.E.) echo in characterizations of humanity as
naturally brutal, quarrelsome, miserable, and in desperate need

of law. In Plato's *Protagoras*, the sophist of that name identifies the sense of "justice" as the only human survival equipment that counts. Notions that justice could be independent of or in actual opposition to the state were in tiny infancy. Certainly in the popular mind, the city-state alone offered salvation, and the state was glad to reinforce this conviction by claimed contacts with the gods (oaths, sacrifices, curses, other ceremonies) and supervision of private religious functions like the Eleusinian mysteries.

Athenians had a particularly high regard for their city-state, and their emotional and practical investment in it was huge. Never passive patriots, they thought of participation in government as a man's proper daily occupation. Some much-cited evidence of this is the origin of our word "idiot." *Idios* is the Greek word for "private person," or one who minds his own business. In Athens, this could be an insult. Many conventions confirmed the expectation of civic activity. For example, men were herded out of the marketplace into the Assembly in the morning with a rope soaked in vermilion, which gave stragglers a mark of shame on their clothes. Even more emphatic were the public arts. Thucydides shows Pericles orating at a funeral for war dead, urging the crowd to contemplate Athens, to become lovers of Athens (*The Peloponnesian War* 2.43), and he apparently offended no one with the implication that the mourners had not already sacrificed plenty. What made the Athenians such junkies of government? The sketch of history that follows may help explain.

In the same speech in Thucydides, Athens is made out to be the original Greek democracy (2.37), and nothing contradicts this. There is, indeed, much to back it up. According to the ancients, one notable feature of Athenian history was autochthony, or the fact that the race had always been there; this was unusual in the Greek world, where people moved around like game pieces sliding and rattling in a box. The Athenians had certainly not, as they imagined, been there since the beginning of humankind, but their settlements are prehistoric, and the momentous Dorian invasion of the eleventh century B.C.E. missed their territory altogether. In the Greek world, more overrunning made for more authoritarianism; typically, an invading Dorian population turned the natives into a subject people who could never get out from under their masters. The people of Attica, although they were far from a classless society, did not have ethnic differences reinforcing their divisions. Relative homogeneity must have contributed to more trust and interdependence and thus to democracy.

Another fairly unusual feature of Athenian politics is *synoecismus* ("living together"). In remote times, independent political centers were scattered all over Attica; Eleusis, which through myth retained memories of royalty into the historical period, was only one of the centers. The myth about the Athenian king Theseus uniting Attica says nothing about force, and this is borne out by people never (as far as anyone can now tell) having suffered diminished rights or privileges because of birthplace or place of residence. (Qualified citizens only had to make it to Athens to take part in the government, a hardship treated jokingly in the first scene of *Lysistrata*.) The process of union was probably peaceful and gradual. That Attica consented to "live together" (while most other regions kept separate city-states or created loose federations), and then faced the problems of including such a scattered citizenry, doubtless conduced strongly to democracy.

Athens did have typical social stratification and typical social stresses, and the government might have remained dominated by nobility and wealth, or takeovers might have stuck. (The Greeks called these "tyrannies," not to indicate malign character necessarily, but irregularity: these were not oligarchies or inherited monarchies, but impromptu one-man governments; the Greeks therefore applied an Eastern name to the at first unfamiliar, un-Greek institution.) But Athens had unusual insight in recognizing trouble and unusual prudence in accepting reorganization, with the powerful ceding some of their interests in the name of long-term stability. At early stages, certainly, the Athenians had a justified confidence in creating better government.

Draco was lawgiver perhaps in 621/620 B.C.E. Solon's political leadership may have started around 600 B.C.E., and some years later he was chosen as a special constitutional arbitrator. He dealt with an economic emergency by canceling debts and promoting trade. He made officeholding dependent on income instead of family descent, as previously. The archonship or highest magistracy was now open to any citizen who could fulfill a wealth qualification, and men of moderate means were eligible for lower offices. Either now or somewhat earlier, the *thetes*, or those with an income as low as nil, could act in the Assembly, and he established under the Assembly's authority

the prototype of the popular court. Other of Solon's arrangements are cloudier but probably included the creation or reform
of executive structures.

These measures earned Solon a title to statesmanship he has
not lost to this day. ("Local Solons Meet," reads the headline of a
small-town newspaper.) But for the immediate future, what he
had achieved was either too much at once, or too little too late, or
maybe an illustration of the impracticality of the middle of the
road. The nation snapped promptly into literal anarchy: during
several years (we do not know which ones, but they occurred in
the 580s B.C.E.) there were no archons. But the takeover by a tyrant
around twenty years later was, rather than a further blow to democratic development, a means of bringing it about more quickly.

As in the modern world, authoritarian figures in Greece and
Rome could have a paradoxical status. Often they rose due to
popular acclaim and represented the common people better than
a previous oligarchy had. They were not necessarily hard to
depose, and when they did go, they might leave the elite, govern-
ing class with a higher standard for attention to the needs of the
poor. Pisistratus took up the cause of the Hill party, consisting not
only of hardscrabble highlanders but of the urban poor. He had
to seize power three times, by different stratagems (once, according to legend, he disguised a tall peasant girl as Athena to act as
his sponsor), but when established he conducted himself fairly
beneficently up until his death in 527 B.C.E. Representative offices
continued to function; he only pulled strings. His land distribu-
tions were extensive and a great relief of need, and his rangy,
opportunistic foreign policy spread Athens' power and opened
up new trade routes.

Pisistratus came up with a quintessentially Athenian mix of
pork-barrel and propaganda in the form of buildings and festi-
vals. One relevant festival was not even Athenian, but of the distant island of Delos, where Ionian Greeks from Asia Minor
celebrated the birth of Apollo. Pisistratus had Apollo's temple
precinct cleared of graves, thereby giving Athens symbolic
patronage of the festival; Athens already had the status of mother
city of the Ionian colonies. The tyrant (or his son Hipparchus)
also founded contests in Homeric recitation at the Panathenaea
festival in Athens, institutionalizing Homer, who had come from
somewhere in Asia Minor and written in the Ionian dialect of
which Attic was a newer form, as the archetypal literary genius.

These moves helped to square off, in the popular mind, what was in reality a pretty fuzzy, long-diversified ethnic group, the Ionians, against another one almost equally so, the Dorians. A lot of what members of each group believed they had in common with each other actually consisted of propagandistic reconstructions. Sad. In effect, leaders were already preparing for the Peloponnesian War.

As is often the case, the one-man government show proved awkward to pass down. Pisistratus' sons lost out to aristocratic rivalry and their own nasty performance, leaving the government again to figure out what to do with itself. In 508/507 B.C.E. Cleisthenes reformed the administration of Athens considerably by an ingenious reshuffle. The four ancient Ionian tribes had been the basis of representation, with a hundred men from each serving on the Council of Four Hundred. This made for factionalism, because the clans operating within the tribes all had their separate interests. Cleisthenes introduced a new federal system, but not with straightforward geographical divisions, which would have left substantial pressure groups intact. He instead created ten new tribes, each consisting of three groups of demes (administrative areas): one group from the coast, one from Athens or its surroundings, and one from inland. Fifty men, a certain number from each deme according to its size, represented each new tribe each year on the new Council of Five Hundred. Each fifty would take a turn as the steering committee for a tenth part of the year. These fifty were the "presidents" or *prytaneis*, so that the committee serving at any one time was called the Prytany Council. During the initial years of the reform, a preliminary election in the demes seems to have supplied candidates for a lottery, but a few decades later lottery alone staffed the Council of Five Hundred. It would have been much harder now to promote an interest group, in a temporary, randomly chosen contingent with two thirds of which one had little in common, and factionalism within the government probably did weaken.

From 501/500 B.C.E., the Cleisthenic tribes began to elect one general each, and this popular election was to take on great importance a few years later when the commander-in-chief came to be chosen by lot. It being unsustainable for an office so prone to mediocre incumbents to maintain its considerable power, the power slipped away to the elected generals, who were to play vivid roles in a government where official position usually meant obscurity.

Popular history credits Cleisthenes with introducing ostracism; at any rate, ostracism was practiced a couple of decades later, as archeologists confirm through their finds of hundreds of pottery shards (*ostraka*) with names etched on them. During an ostracism, citizens could vote for the ten-year expulsion of any citizen they wished, on any or no grounds. (The usual grounds were that someone was gaining enough influence to threaten a political balance.) Six thousand votes cast constituted the legal threshold for the ostracism to take effect, and the man with the most votes was condemned. Ostracism was a yearly opportunity presented to the Assembly, but after a fad in the 480s B.C.E., people were not as enthusiastic. But the possibility of abrupt exile did continue to serve the purpose of discouraging wealthy and prominent men from negotiating Athens' political future privately with domestic and foreign powers alike. Ostracism lasted almost until the final decade of the fifth century.

From 487 B.C.E. onward, even the archonships were filled by lottery. Under the leadership of Ephialtes (early to middle fifth century B.C.E.) and Pericles (c. 495–429 B.C.E.), Athens completed its radical democracy. Ephialtes deprived the aristocratic Council of the Areopagus of all its powers except to try homicides and similar crimes, and all other jurisdiction fell to the popular court. Pericles opened the archonship to a lower income group and introduced pay for officeholders, including jurors. In line with his populist program, he was a hawk. Because the government was strongly redistributive, the internal resources of Attica could never have sufficed for the workfare and welfare and public facility commitments of the regime, including the Parthenon and its massive gold and ivory statue of Athena. Athens had to exploit its empire single-mindedly through tribute and other impositions, although this was one thing that led to rebellions. At this point we are in the Peloponnesian War.

The health of the completed system has come under attack by certain aristocratic and antidemocratic writers (among whom perhaps Aristophanes should be counted), though this does not mean that the system was healthy. Even if it wasn't, it would seem rather cruel to pass, as these writers sometimes do, moral judgment on the Athenian populace, the poorest of whom were clothes-on-their-back, rudimentary-shelter, maybe-enough-food-for-today poor. It is hardly amazing that they fought to get and keep government benefits. Moreover, many of their measures have the look of reactions to dismal treatments under previous governments. But understandable motivations did not mitigate the character of the radical democracy, which like many revolutionary regimes recapitulated in more-damaging forms the abuses it intended to suppress forever. But before I go on, I must stress that I am not a historian, much less an expert on the poorly attested and controversial nature of the Classical Athenian state. I can only record my impressions, based on the facts but admittedly sympathetic to Aristophanes.

Elitist factionalism could not be cured by the exclusion of elitist factions. Aristophanes' own proposal for coping with oligarchical cliques without some change in the system is flaky: they're like mats in raw wool, so card them out and pluck their heads off (577f.). The clubs were nothing like tangles in the fiber of the state; the democracy had long ago made them an alien substance. How could the government, without violence or repression, control forces outside of its official self, forces to whom it could offer no incentives for good behavior? Elites have a natural expectation of participating in government, and Athens' elite became viciously frustrated in its long exclusion from campaigning for anything but generalships and diplomatic appointments. Wealthy young men did not systematically prepare for political office, because it was unlikely that any individual would hold one for more than a few weeks, no matter how well he prepared. (Aristocratic young Roman men, after an intensive education in rhetoric and an administrative apprenticeship, took up elective offices in a fixed order, each one serving as training for the next.) Instead, leisured youth roamed around town with Socrates, listening to him explain how obvious it was that the "best" people should govern, while a popular dramatist like Aristophanes could get away with maintaining that Athens actually detested its "good" citizens (*Frogs* 1455f.). When Critias and his friends came to power as the Thirty Tyrants after the coup of 404 B.C.E., they turned with alacrity to killing democrats and moderates. Privileged groups are selfish, but when properly integrated into a government, they evolve a selfish interest in competence, order, and stability. And when the privileged operate in a sanctioned system, it is easier to keep control of them.

The system did not provide even for popular leadership to operate officially. Since government officeholding was in a forum of forced and obscure cooperation, charismatic people gained power by speaking in the Assembly and prosecuting in the courts. The reckless Cleon, whom Aristophanes loathed, was a "leader of the people," or demagogue. (*Knights* is a whole play about demagoguery: Cleon is an evil new pet slave of Demos ["The People"] and terrorizes the whole household until deposed by a sausage-seller.) We naturally read more about the scandalously bad advisors of the citizen body than about useful and informative speakers, but there does seem to have been a tendency for Athenians to reward those demagogues who spoke with all the responsibility and restraint of casino ads and later to display the rage of someone who has blown a month's food budget on slot machines. Athenian politics exudes an air of goofiness partly because of the detachment of so many players from administrative reality. An officeholder in a political system more like our own at least gains over time some sense of possibilities and probabilities. In *Lysistrata*, the Councilor's description of the proposal to make war on Sicily (387ff.) parodies decision-making frippery in the radical democracy.

That the government functioned with reasonable efficiency is a testament to the prevalence of literacy and public spirit in Attica. Moreover, political corruption often being a function of long-term connections, coming to an office unexpectedly must have lessened the chances of exploiting it shrewdly, Aristophanes' constant complaints about graft notwithstanding. Lines 490f. and 577f. of *Lysistrata*, in condemning abuses, actually give hints of how challenging they were. Those who may come across to a modern reader as electoral hopefuls were most likely winners of offices by lot who had to stir up trouble *before* their tenures in order to skim from fines and profit from other measures during the cleanup. As to how successful the corrupt might be, it should be kept in mind that some astute rules combated mismanagement: independent government bodies confirmed appointments and audited tenure, and skilled slaves, whose loyalty was necessarily to their owner, the state, gave administrative support.

But this seems a cumbersome apparatus for what elections could by and large have achieved. The apparatus can look a little like a carnival ride, designed to give a long line of ticketholders the brief thrill of "driving" a vehicle whose steering wheel doesn't work. Government as entertainment was not a good deal. Mediocrity was a general drag on the city-state's ambitions.

Moreover, scantily gifted citizens prizing the equal chance to hold office were aware of the rarity and fragility of the setup, and they evolved a politics of touchy jealousy. Aristophanes' Chorus of Old Men may be paranoid within the economy of the comedy, but within the economy of history such people knew what they were talking about. They *were* prone to losing their privileges. They *had* to treat anything outstanding with suspicion.

An anecdote illustrates egalitarian potshots in Athens. Aristides, who had been a commander at the Battle of Marathon and was styled the Just, once wrote his own name on a ballot for ostracism at the request of an illiterate man and asked him why he wanted Aristides ostracized. "Because I am sick of hearing him called the Just," the man answered. Episode after episode of Athenian history glides before the reader's eyes, with a series of creative, even brilliant generals. But hardly any seem to have been able to retire in calm and esteem. A notable number, driven away, went over to the enemy of the time. Pericles, with his long tenure, was a great exception, but toward the end of his life he was prosecuted and fined, and had he lived a few years longer, Athens would have gotten him decisively, I am sure. There was little balance in considering generals' successes against their failures, and little account taken of circumstances outside their control. Six of those commanding at the great naval victory at Arginusae in 406 B.C.E. were put to death later because a storm had prevented them from fishing survivors from their own side out of the water. This was only the culmination of abuse of authority—in the opposite of its usual sense. For a long time, the state had simply been throwing away talent.

Then there is the question of money. Aristophanes' most frequent political complaint is that people cannot keep their snouts out of the trough. The democracy could not have blossomed without salaries and stipends to allow everyone to take time off work. (Starting late in the fifth century even attendance at the Assembly was paid.) But had the range of services paid for been less generous—more in line with what the state needed than with what unemployed people wanted to perform—the outcome would have been better. The need for and the cost of the navy were intertwined: the triremes had to ensure their continuing finance by patrolling the empire. The trial courts, on the other hand, were essential in basic function but very wasteful in their setup. That there are twelve jurors in Aeschylus' *Eumenides* does not say anything about a standard jury size; jurors for a single case could number a thousand or more, each of them earning a sum that was somewhere around a subsistence wage. Some men connived to double dip by registering for more than one tribunal at a time. In Aristophanes' *Wasps*, a son locks up his father, who is addicted to jury service. The old man proves unconfinable ("I'm smoke coming out the chimney," 144), except when he gets the chance to sit in judgment over two dogs in his own household.

In this play and others, Aristophanes brands the legal system as self-serving and merciless. He undoubtedly exaggerates, but the Athenian law courts do seem to have epitomized one evil of overparticipation in public life: people treating politics as a career were liable to turn procedures, like prosecutions, that should have been only recourses of necessity, into expeditions for profit, influence, revenge, and so on. This is of course a fault of professional politicians everywhere, but imagine a large part of the population becoming professional politicians. And imagine these people, with no legal training and with only loose procedural guidelines, even having the power to rescind laws as unconstitutional and to punish these laws' proposers.

The nadir of sliminess in Aristophanes' depictions is the sycophant ("fig-shower"), a man who sniffed out trivial contraband in order to prosecute the possessor for an official reward or shake him down for a bribe. The sycophant stood for a contingent of informers, who would have had no opportunities had the state not reached far into an individual's life. Diligence, frugality, chastity, and other family obligations; ritual observance and purity; the details of military and civic performance; the satire of a playwright—none of this was considered private or protected in the first place. The radical democracy supplied the machinery to grind any of it to a pulp. And as it was not culturally congenial to limit the state's activities, abuses like sycophancy simply (or not simply—complicatedly) provoked laws to deal with themselves in turn. Official interventions grew in layers.

It did not help that the police were not law enforcers or investigators (but merely keepers of order at public gatherings and bodyguards for officials—both functions appear in *Lysistrata*), or that the state's role in prosecution was occasional, and in defense nonexistent. Private people had to act for themselves, and an immense arrogance arose from the lack of distinction between the state's interests and one's own motives.

Old Comedy repeatedly encapsulated the persecution citizens were vulnerable to. Plays show government-sanctioned pests—pressure groups, officials, informers, soothsayers—trying to stop healthy political acting up or raid preparations for a feast. In *Lysistrata*, the veterans and the Councilor are the intruders. Even discounting Aristophanes' comic mania, something disturbing is visible here. Things were too open; competition was too hectic. Political agents in their great numbers and wide spheres had little sense of natural limits, little incentive to learn "shame," as the Greeks called the vital quality of self-limitation.

This carried over to foreign policy, in which the democrats could not manage to treat other states with even self-protective accommodation. Athenians refused generous peace offers at times of Spartan weakness. The pre-Christian ethics of revenge and suspicious looking out for one's own normally created wide polarizations in Greek politics, but the Athenians were the real pros.

The comedy of *Lysistrata* is somewhat pathetic in the final scenes, where Aristophanes imagines that the Greeks—especially the Athenians—can be utterly changed to merit another future. The prospect of losing forever that most satisfying coming together of difference, sex, has panicked the Spartan government, Cinesias, the Council, and the Ambassadors into leaping straight to a deal. The negotiation scene (1106ff.) is a short, absurd tale of extremist cooperation. The parties can barely take in the sermonizing against squabbling, so aroused are they by nude Reconciliation. They make brain-numb stabs at defending old positions and then agree to peace in mere anticipation of unspecified territorial compromises. *Lysistrata* is like a mother's fantasy of pouring bourbon into toddlers to keep them from whacking each other with their toys. Sadly, there is no evidence that the play did anything to hasten the peace.

Commentary 2

Ancient Greek Warfare

It is hard to read *Lysistrata* right, if a major purpose of reading it is to learn about its author's world. One special danger is to read into it a pacifism that Aristophanes would have found sentimental or fanatical.

Warfare in ancient Greece was not a profession or an isolated enterprise, but a common way of life. If trade and intellectual life made Greeks cheerful and forward-looking, warfare made them gloomy. In Sophocles' tragedy *Oedipus at Colonus*, the thesis (familiar in Greek literature) that the best thing for a human being is not to exist at all rests mainly on the certainty of war: revolutions, strife, battles, and slaughter are listed along with old age as expected parts of the life cycle (1230ff.).

As in a number of other traditional societies, the gender division of labor dictated that men fought—that was for the Greeks part of the definition of a man. The graphic symbols that we inherit from this culture show a hand mirror for female and a round shield with a spear projecting from behind it for male. The city-state usually exempted slaves from military service on the grounds that they did not have a sufficient stake in the polity to be good fighters. But with a few exceptions for practical purposes, male citizens and resident aliens served in the army, and training and equipping youth were ordinary tasks of families and communities, who seem never to have disputed the contribution of fighting to health, beauty, and "character." (Plato goes as far as to state that fortifications are decadent because they take away opportunities for combat [*Laws* 6.778Df.].) The start of soldiering was so well integrated into the rituals of growing up a free male that resistance was unknown; it would have been resistance to growing up itself, and to all of the privileges a free man enjoyed. Men accepted military duties in the hard conditions of the ancient Mediterranean, even though liability for call-up extended to the age of sixty; and even though there was essentially nothing but frontlines, patrols, or garrisons to be drafted into: there were no relatively safe logistical units, no military bureaucracy at home—only war, or war on the verge of happening.

Lysistrata nowhere suggests that warfare in itself is intolerable, let alone immoral. The women make war on a small scale, and the song at the end celebrates military victory. In some of his other plays, Aristophanes picks on the notorious coward Cleonymus unmercifully. I have no reason not to believe that he shared his fellow citizens' idea of an army as an inseparable part of a civilized state, the kind of state that could bless human beings with law. Neither, on the other hand, was the playwright unusual in opposing a policy of aggression against neighbors and recommending cooperation. This opinion belonged to many of the wealthier, more conservative people at the time. The Greeks were by no means mindlessly warlike, and peace treaties were a long-standing part of foreign policy. This was because military policy was integral to regular politics. In Athens, generals were elected and military campaign plans debated freely and decided on democratically; those people with special knowledge of strategy were the glorified errand boys of the majority (and were subject to prompt *de*glorification and punishment when they failed). It was therefore normal to question the value or direction of a war, and the Peloponnesian War had been controversial since its inception. Probably no one but the extraordinarily charismatic Pericles could have seen this conflict beyond its awful early years, with the destruction of the Attic countryside and the plague within Athens. Aristophanes had every right and even obligation to speak his mind. The daring absurdity of the *Lysistrata* story consists in the women, sick of men's bungling, taking on military policy themselves.

Within this narrow farcical framework, Aristophanes manages to say some interesting things about the role of the military in public life. But before exploring this, I need to tell briefly how the Greeks came to this point in their military history.

We know of only one Greek society that, on the evidence, was peaceful, the Minoans of Crete, and there is some debate about whether we can even call them Greeks. They had a lush palace culture devoted to parties and sports. None of their surviving art depicts warfare. Instead, women's open, breast-framing bodices shout, "Make love, not war!" (to those of us brought up on such slogans, anyway). Around the middle of the second millennium B.C.E., volcanic eruption or takeover by the Mycenaean Greeks of the mainland destroyed their civilization, and that was that.

The Mycenaeans *were* warlike. Palace records inventory arma-
ments, which are found in abundance in tombs as well. In the
Homeric poems, reaching back into the Mycenaean period
(which ended around 1100 B.C.E.), Greek men are soldiers, or
rather warriors, a term that stresses individualism. Homer
depicts a system of noble clans spread over the eastern Mediterranean. With its emphasis on personal prestige and on raiding
cattle, women, and other commodities, the society had certain
similarities to the tribes of pastoral Africa. A fully initiated young
African man may identify himself as a warrior even though his
tribe never fights what we would call wars. Only under the
empire of the Zulu Shaka was fighting tightly bound up with the
state. Before and after that, to raid and to meet for sportsmanlike
"battles" have meant more or less to display personal bravery
and to enrich oneself. The extension of a modern sort of political
power has hardly been part of the thinking.

The warrior of the Homeric poems is comparable. Although he
belongs to a fighting group, he zooms around the battlefield on
his chariot at will, as if he is shopping in a bargain basement.
When he sees someone he wishes to fight (perhaps an old rival),
he stops, dismounts, and uses a throwing spear, a sword, and
heavy armor in single combat. A slain enemy is "stripped," or
relieved of all of his valuable equipment, and transformed into
part of his emulous enemy's stats. Foot soldiery and archery in
Homer imply undifferentiated targets, as on modern battlefields.
But the duel for glory and goodies has centrality. Achilles,
Agamemnon, and others in the *Iliad* have their private empires in
the camp, collections of prizes (tripod cauldrons, women slaves,
cattle) through which they compete with each other for status.
And these competitions appear to mean far more than state
authority does. Achilles, the best fighter, asserts that if he cannot
keep prizes in proportion to his deeds, he is not interested in
fighting any more for Agamemnon, who is a king and the leader
of all the assembled Greek troops. Achilles goes on strike, and
Agamemnon is eventually forced to give in. The Trojan War,
which did take place in some form, is sometimes called "the real
First World War," but nothing like later wars was probably happening in the Greek world at the time. Probably no big, splashy
aims like conquest of territory figured in fighting. In Homer, the
city of Troy is sacked after a long siege, but the winners simply
kill the men, enslave the women, and go home. The archeological

evidence seconds this: the city, once it passed through a violent catastrophe (around 1200 B.C.E.), went into such sharp material decline that it is hard to believe the conquerors had moved in and were making use of it.

It was evidently in this somewhat whimsically organized state of affairs, rather than later when warfare was a matter of more rigid policy, that ideas recognizable to us as pacifist arose. Material things have finite value. It is natural to question the risk of irreplaceable human life in the quest for trophies and trinkets. In the *Iliad*, Achilles refuses to stop sulking and return to battle when he is first offered what he originally demanded and much more. It is as if the days of sitting in his tent, already surrounded by fine things, have made him ask what all of this is about. The speech he makes to Agamemnon's emissaries excites modern pacifists.

> To me life is not to be traded for everything they say
> The well-built city of Ilium acquired
> In peace before the Achaeans came;
> Nor everything the stone shrine
> Of the archer Phoebus Apollo contains at rocky Pytho.
> Cattle and fat sheep can be taken as plunder.
> Tripods and tawny-headed horses can be bought.
> But a man's breath cannot be plundered back
> Or retaken, once it has passed the barrier of his teeth.   (9.401ff.)

The imagery unrelieved by abstraction is typical of the *Iliad*. The poet never indulges in any equivocation on the subject of war: you can *die* in it, your skull shattered and brain mashed, entrails pierced, limbs hacked; whereas later authors were absorbed in strategy and politics and almost never touched on what happens to the bodies of individuals. The early Greeks, if Homer gives an accurate impression, saw war in its nitty-gritty and could feel accordingly unhappy with it. The women in Homer have not got a good word to say about war. In the *Odyssey*, when Odysseus meets Achilles in the Underworld, he postulates that the young man's ghost must find comfort in both his glorious forfeited life as a fighter and his high status now. Achilles says he would rather be the living slave of a serf than king of all the dead (11.482ff.).

The Greek world, however, did not develop further these moving ideas and put them into practice. One reason was the rise of the city-state and the rule of law, which were more than popu-

lar—they were worshiped. (Justice was a goddess.) The armies
that eventually replaced freebooting gangs took on some of the
holy aura of legitimate government. Homeric careerism had
faded, and a sense of duty to the community ruled instead. The
willing loss of husbands, fathers, and sons was part of this duty,
mitigated by the thanks and support the state offered.

The colonies the city-states started sending out late in the Dark
Ages helped establish these ethics. Colonies let the Greeks
emerge from overpopulated misery to spacious opportunity, but
very few of the Mediterranean's islands or mainland shores were
uninhabited to start with. A colonial expedition had to have a
good enough military to scatter or suppress the natives perma-
nently. Trained militias with efficient call-up arrangements
would have worked best. That Greeks made war against "barbarians" for the very existence of cities played a big role in sanctify-
ing the state's use of organized force.

Defeated "barbarians," mostly people of rudimentary technol-
ogy, did not furnish much loot beyond their own persons as
slaves; anyway, it was chiefly the land the colonists were after.
Striving to capture a particularly splendid set of arms from a fellow Greek as a major purpose of fighting was outdated as well
(although looting definitely persisted). The state made serving in
standard sets of armor a condition of participating in the government at different levels, and certain types of governments and
certain types of armies were mutually reinforcing. The aristocratic government of Thessaly was associated with a strong cavalry, made up of the citizens rich enough to supply themselves
with horses. Hoplite ("shielded") troops were prominent in
looser oligarchies, like those of the Peloponnese. Hoplite armor
was affordable to middle- or upper-middle-class people (to use
our only tenuously applicable terms). The evolution of radical
democracy in Athens is bound up with the growth of the city as a
naval power. Rowers were the manpower of the powerful trireme
warships, and all the equipment a rower needed was a leather
"oar-loop," a special pillow on which to slide forward and back-
ward on the bench while rowing, and an oar; *Lysistrata* itself contains evidence (421f.) that the state supplied at least the oar.
Paupers could serve in the navy, and Athens came to pay them
well and to depend on them to police its empire.

But Aristophanes might have agreed that the thorough integration of the military into the state and the consequent reverence

for the military as an institution did little to ensure that the military was used ethically. Leaders took it for granted that armies would live off enemy land and massacre or sell the defeated unless it were more profitable to ransom them or strategically more advantageous to hang onto them. To some extent, the city-state was an outsized bandit. Hoplite armies were effective enough to make large territorial conquests. Hoplites advanced in a tight, layered formation, helmeted, corsleted, greaved, holding up large, convex shields by well-balanced grips, and thrusting with long spears. It was like a spiked steamroller. But one break in the line could be disastrous; armies had to gain in discipline. When discipline combined with traditional Greek courage, and generals got an idea of the best ways to position and move this force, there was nothing like hoplites in the known world. (The potentates of the east had great enthusiasm for hoplite mercenaries. Xenophon's *Anabasis* [*The March Inland*] is an entertaining account of getting such an army out of Asia Minor after the collapse of a campaign.)

Sparta used a hoplite army to take extensive land from neighbors, retake it after a rebellion, and keep it (despite more outbreaks) for centuries, apparently on the sole pretext that the proceeds of this land, which was worked by serfs called helots, supported the totalitarian military machine needed to keep it. During the seventh-century B.C.E. Second Messenian War, which repressed the first rebellion, the poet and general Tyrtaeus single-mindedly goaded Spartan soldiers to greater bravery. He would not mention a man in song, he writes, for the most sublime athletic prowess, beauty, wealth, kingly power, or eloquence (strange item, coming from a poet)—but for courage only, since this alone means glory (Fragment 9). The system that solidified in the following generations was obsessively militaristic beyond anything the modern world has seen. Mothers surrendered their sons to barracks at the age of seven. Law, politics, and social and family life—all served the military.

If hoplite armies overshadowed the plains in the historical period, navies dominated the sea. The trireme was, like the hoplite, an innovation that would not take no for an answer. This vessel was large and fast enough to sink without ado the ships it rammed with its metal beak, but small enough, given an experienced commander and crew, to maneuver slyly even in narrow straits. (Rowers' discipline was to keep strict pace with each other, according to a musical beat provided, and to obey commands instantly.) Small fleets could therefore sometimes defeat much larger ones, and marine tactics developed rapidly.

The growth of Athens' power was, from an early date, connected to the sea. Around the beginning of the sixth century B.C.E., for example, Solon egged his countrymen on to take the island of Salamis from the coastal city of Megara, and they did so. The Delian League, a protective alliance formed in the aftermath of the Persian invasions of 490 and 480–479 B.C.E., became by diplomatic sleight of hand the administrative basis of the Athenian naval empire. Whichever states did not make a navy available for the Athenians to command had to pay for their "protection." The navies kept order, but at the cost of the freedom of sea routes, so that Athens could almost name its cut of the eastern Mediterranean's trade in the form of tribute, imposts, and monopolies. Foreign traders within the empire could not even be sure of the protection of law, because their lawsuits with Athenians were adjudicated at Athens. Athens exercised inordinate political influence as well, especially in setting up puppet democratic regimes. Some allies and subject states were unhappy enough to turn for precarious refuge to the Spartan sphere, and this was a major cause of the Peloponnesian War.

But I am getting ahead of myself, and I need to sketch more of the background to the war, after repeating my proviso that I am not a historian, only a writer looking at the historical facts in light of Aristophanes. To changes I have already described was added the idea of new moral purpose in warfare, something beyond the welfare of a single city-state. Like much of the globe in the late twentieth century, the Greek world of the late fifth century B.C.E. had experienced a "good war," or rather two, the Persian Wars just cited. Both World War II and the Persian Wars were fought against ruthless and tyrannical enemies. In either case, the aggression was so well organized and on such a giant scale that it threatened a large part of the world with an unhappy future and forced even the cynical into moral judgment. A number of Greek states cooperated to fight the Persians in the second struggle, putting aside their feuds and their normally divergent interests; many individuals behaved with great nobility, and the beauty of their stories still moves us, if only because the chronicler Herodotus lays it on so thick. (Never mind: while sure of his exaggerations, historians concede that the Greeks were far outnumbered, that the

Spartans died to a man at Thermopylae, and that several other inspiring things are true in their essentials.) The soldier sacrificed himself to the state—this was not new. But now the state's purposes in going to war had an added worth: not only to acquire, retain, or be safe, but also to preserve a way of life it believed to be a precious gift of the gods: Greekness. The Greeks of the fifth century B.C.E. had the beginnings of ethnic nationalism. Nothing could be clearer than the final song in *Lysistrata:* the Greeks must be mindful of the blessing of having fought and won together.

But one great difference between the Greeks and other language-sharing groups made trouble for the Athenians' struggle to force a continuance of their anti-Persian alliance as an empire. The Greeks had previously gone so far out of their way to fight together not to achieve political union (Philip of Macedon would force a federation on them around a century and a half later only with great strain), but to keep the opposite: the right of each city-state to govern itself as it saw fit. To be Greek entailed living in a city-state whose form of government and outside commitments were freely chosen. (Or this was the theory. In reality, interventionist politics went back hundreds of years—but at least had greater limits in the more limited power of the meddling states.) Although this was certainly not the only incitement for the Peloponnesian War, Athens' imposition of oppressive conditions on its allies, and its simultaneous claim to moral leadership because of its military leadership in the Persian Wars, must have looked pretty revolting. Aristophanes' stance in *Lysistrata* is consistent: when Athenian "patriots" boast of past military achievement in order to get their own way in the present, they are merely being obnoxious. Only when at the end of the play the Athenians and Spartans rejoice in joint historical victories does martial pride have meaning.

Athens had set itself up so that the war, once started, had to escalate—city-states by their very nature resisted domination, so the means to control them had to grow in brutality, but without any sober hope on Athens' part of a final triumph. Sparta was always going to be there and would always fight Athens' claims; the individual character of states after long periods of separate development had effected this too: Sparta was the state that had gone all-out for the military. Sparta was the unbreakable pit in the fruit of Greece. Sparta would win, but it took a long time for its traditional discipline to face down Athens' frustrated pride and rage. It took even more time in that Sparta the land power and Athens the sea power both avoided slugging it out decisively; neither side was willing to campaign in a format in which its preparation was mediocre.

Thucydides writes at the beginning of his *Peloponnesian War* that from the onset he could tell this was going to be an unprecedented conflict, and he is someone to listen to. He was an Athenian general in the war, and he spent the years after his forced retirement in exile, compiling his masterpiece of military history, which included campaigns in which he himself had taken part. Whether in fact Thucydides is as accurate as he claims to be—a subject on which scholars disagree—his exemplary care in detail and his distaste for Herodotean exaggeration help convince us that the war was as wearing as he says it was ("never before had so many cities been captured and destroyed . . . never had there been so many exiles, never so many fatalities" [1.23]) and that Aristophanes had far more reasons than he states openly for wanting it to end. The playwright's fiercest depiction of the sufferings of the war belongs to his youthful work *Acharnians*, with the little girls eager to be sold into slavery so that they do not starve (731ff.). But even at the mellower stage of *Lysistrata*, he insists that things are wrong. He shows, for example, that the scheduling of warfare is changing to allow more distant and ruthless persecution. Calonice complains that her husband has been gone for five months, Myrrhine that hers has been away for seven, Lampito that hers hardly pauses at home (102ff.). This would not have been the case in an old-fashioned war with a campaigning season of summer only: invade, sack, spend the rest of the year with the family. War was becoming abnormal.

Because Athens and Sparta fought mostly through their respective allies, this, not the Trojan War, was the prototype of a world war, fought on many fronts and drawing in many states and various ethnic groups (the Persians and other non-Greeks got involved). The war was longer (431–404 B.C.E.) than any previous one on record, and of greater geographical extent (from the Hellespont to Sicily). Whole nations were displaced or eliminated.

Moreover, the Greeks were close enough to each other in a variety of ways that this was a sort of civil war too, with a civil war's typical agony. The Greek world, patrolled by the Athenians, had been trading and cultivating other associations at a great clip. The legally enforced racial exclusivity of the Athenian and the Spartan citizenships created only limited isolation. Guest-friendship, intermarriage, and colonization (with some colonies later sending out colonies of their own) ensured a great many close ties across the barriers of city-states anyway. The ancient great athletic games Lysistrata mentions (1129ff.) also saw the different city-states cooperating. Gorgias the sophist declared that Greeks should mourn, not erect trophies, after defeating other Greeks (Diels Fragment II 82 [76] 5b).

We have little information about personal experiences in the war, but the traditional wisdom about civil wars appears deeply true of this one: there is no hatred like the hatred among relatives. Thucydides' history refers again and again to "all kinds of killings"—clearly a euphemism for atrocities carried out on individuals—and is full of accounts of what we would think of as mass violations of human rights; both types of brutality owed something to the intimate entanglements and terrible resentments within and between cities. Athens helped provoke the war with the Megarian Decree of 432 B.C.E. against its neighbor and old rival Megara, a sweeping embargo that had nearly the force of a siege. In 427 B.C.E., in a spree of slaughter, the Corcyrean democrats violated the traditional refuge of a temple precinct to massacre members of an oligarchic party they had stopped in an attempt to overthrow the government. Two years later, they caught the last of the conspirators. These, as if they were concentration camp victims rebelling, refused to leave a building and be marched to their death, so their enemies tore off the roof and competed to kill the prisoners with missiles faster than the prisoners could kill themselves. Genocidal measures after the capitulation of cities seem to have become worse over the course of the war, which suggests, along with growing rage, growing exhaustion: families and states, if they still existed, were too poor to pay ransoms, and the market for slaves was saturated.

In reading the melancholy history of this war, I am reminded of the American Civil War, with the murderous conditions at Andersonville prison camp and Sherman's marauding march through Georgia. It appears to be easier in a civil war to forget about gaining measurable advantages and concentrate on causing suffering and humiliation.

But it is more than refined hatred that makes civil wars so grim. They are especially prone to be fought in the streets, not on battlefields that exclude noncombatants from the actual battles.

Because the city-states were so involved with each other, combat tended to grow out of political intrigue, so that the combat happened where the intrigue had, in the town. The pattern of episodes is almost boring. City A throws out ruling party B, which appeals to more powerful city C, which seeks to restore B to power (C to puppeteer B afterward), but not if City D, the sponsor of the new regime in A, can help it. Cities E, F, and G fight as allies with or send mercenaries to any of the above. The parties to a civil war are, of course, not the only warring parties to work directly on the cities and populations they want to control; but it is far more rare that they meet on some remote plain and march together in a dainty eighteenth-century manner, all the protocols intact. Civil wars are just not structured that way. Too bad for the women and children and old people in them.

To sum up, the Peloponnesian War's horror must have reinforced uneasiness about international violence. Greece had long had the rule of law, which was supposed to make destruction of life more or less the sole right of governments. This rudimentary development alone rendered consulting about the uses of war inevitable. The Greeks had fought just and satisfying wars together against foreign aggressors, so that fighting each other was tinged with guilt. And the present war seemed to prudent people to be out of control. The why and whether of warfare apparently now competed better with the how. Certainly in Aristophanes' head they did. By presenting women, no matter how ridiculously, as agents of military policy, he urges a broadening of considerations in the making of that policy.

This is clearest to me in lines 588ff., where motherhood and military disaster are set side by side. Lysistrata says that women have a stake: they bear sons and send them to war. The Councilor cuts her off and forbids her to "remind [us] of misfortune." ("That spot is sore!" I translate.) A dramatist could be fined for that. What Lysistrata must have in mind is that Athens has recently lost the cream of her army in an excessively stupid expedition to conquer Syracuse, undertaken with the backing of reports (false, it turned out) of local wealth. The Sicilians placed the defeated survivors in an unsheltered stone pit and watched the corpses pile up and rot.

The passage is poignant for other reasons as well. Sicily was not only an agonizing loss but also the point of no return in the war. When *Lysistrata* was presented, key allies of Athens were rebelling, the vital reserve fund of a thousand talents had gone to restore the navy, the Spartans had established a year-round garrison at Decelea, on Attic soil, and an alliance between Persia and Sparta looked imminent. Citizens did not yet know that Persia was broaching to some Athenian leaders an alliance in exchange for the nullification of the constitution.

Yet nothing was discouraging *enough*. Athens had grown hubristic. To use a term the historian Barbara Tuchman applies to the Vietnam War, the Sicilian expedition was folly, a mass self-destructive self-deception. Like Americans of the 1960s looking at the Vietnam War, Athenians needed to ask themselves, "Are we capable of acting in our own interest? Is our government a responsible one?" but most vitally, "What is this war supposed to be about?"

All this is below the play's surface. On the surface is mostly peace = feast. The characters complain about the loneliness and the consumer hardships of war. A party starts up the moment peace is made. The play is a cogent answer to the long-dead Pericles' militarism: we have our pleasures because we fight for them, the statesman had said. You can fight those pleasures into oblivion, says Aristophanes.

Gandhi Aristophanes was not. But he made an important case for an end to hostilities. For a constant proponent of drinking parties, he had a sober understanding of what war was doing to his homeland.

Commentary 3

Athenian Women

In 330 B.C.E., Demosthenes was scolding his fellow Athenians for not acting against the aggressive and ambitious kingdom of Macedonia. In the good old days, he claimed, a man advising submission to Persia had been stoned to death by the men of the city—and his wife by the women (*On the Crown* 204). Whether this double murder really happened is debatable, but its mention gives an idea of the utter dependence of women and at the same time of the utterly separate spheres of the sexes. Demosthenes must have expected (and as the greatest Greek orator he had excellent instincts) that his audience would find nothing disconcerting in a politically powerless wife sharing in her husband's political lynching. Demosthenes also conveyed that such a lynching would naturally be segregated. And indeed, contact between citizen men and women not related by blood or marriage was not allowed. The intimacy of unisex mob violence would have been taboo. The women would have had to stone their own victim, although how they could manage this in their confined circumstances is anybody's guess. Can you stone someone indoors?

The condition of Athenian women needs a careful approach, so that we do not bury this group under our own concerns—respect for Athenian political and cultural achievements on the one hand, modern feminism on the other. Athenian women were unique in the history of the world. Their oppression and their privileges had a special and deeply Athenian character.

Readers who pursue this topic will run across some scholars, mostly of previous generations, who downplay Athenian women's plight on little more evidence than the strong female characters in myth and some expressions of respect for women within the household. On that logic, the women of rural India have nothing to complain about; goddesses show an idealization of the feminine, and women's domestic roles are acknowledged as important. When we look at modern oppression of women and see how much our knowledge of it depends on their access to the media, it is hard not to conclude the opposite of the more cheerful view of Athenian women's treatment. Women, who could almost never speak for themselves or each other, probably had it worse than we know. The hints we get through men about women's treatment are bad enough in themselves, such as when the character Calonice in *Lysistrata* objects that refusing sex to husbands will get her and the other women beaten and raped (159ff.).

On the radical side of the topic are authors like Eva Keuls in *The Reign of the Phallus*, who identify with Athenian women, take their part, and blame Athenian men, as if in a political campaign over the fate of the living. Framing such writing is a simplistic assumption about how traditional societies work: the strong and evil oppress the weak and good. How far does that get us in our understanding?

What, then, underlay women's condition in Athens? Many scholars, in looking at gender relations there, find it strange and interesting that women were considered naturally wild. It seems self-evident to us that men are biologically more inclined to threaten civilization with violence and promiscuity. The Athenians thought the opposite. Theseus, the mythical founder of Athens, is said to have defeated the female warrior Amazons. The battle was pictured on the frieze of the Parthenon, along with two other key mythical struggles of civilization against barbarity, the Lapiths against the centaurs, and the gods against the giants. In tragedy—another state-sponsored medium—women are prone to every kind of lawless passion. Even the tyrant-defying Antigone, much admired in modern times for her "civil disobedience," would have seemed to her original audience to be an alarming, out of control character, never counting the cost of her actions. The chorus (typically in tragedy the "voice of society") have nervous reservations about her as a martyr. Euripides' heroines—like Medea, who kills her children and her husband's prospective new wife—were such unflattering representatives of the sex that Aristophanes in *Women at the Thesmophoria* depicts women kidnapping the tragedian in revenge. Women are "capable of anything," Lysistrata quotes men as saying (11f.; "cunning to the point of . . . depravity" is my translation), and Calonice heartily agrees. But in the arts lies only a formalization of an attitude we see in ordinary social relations. To marry and start a family was to "tame" a woman and "plow" children. Above all, women were supposed to require locking up and watching, to keep them from indiscriminate sex and other impulsive acts that would destroy their families and the state.

The "problem" of trusting women is a universal one, but other ways of addressing it are more common. Many traditions hold that women are weaker intellectually and morally (as well as physically), but that they are not to blame for what they are and need protection from harm and exploitation. Conservative Moslems think that women, for their own welfare, should have less freedom. Most traditions see women as educable: by learning self-control, they can relieve society from worry about their behavior. Instead of being watched, they can watch themselves, and this means some mobility and autonomy. An ancient example is the Roman matron in her full-length dress, going calmly about her business in public or chattering to men at dinner parties, radiating unavailability.

The Athenians did not exactly say that women had no moral capacity. They had a word, meaning basically "of sound mind," that referred to chaste and decorous character in a woman. But they had no confidence that a woman's good behavior would hold up under pressure. Since it was female nature to be uncontrolled, a woman had, day by day, the potential to run amok and needed a rigidly defined role in the household to channel her energies. To say that marriage (always arranged) was regarded as women's destiny would be an understatement. An unmarried woman lived in tragic limbo, as a living condemnation of her family's failure to give her a future. Marriage was widely thought to contain all of the solutions to the social problems of women (somewhat as childbearing was thought by the medical community to contain most of the solutions to their medical problems). Women's upbringing and their integration into their new homes after marriage reflected this simplistic grasp of their nature. Parents and new husbands preferred to isolate girls rather than persuade them to make the right choices on their own—how many choices would they ever have, after all?

In the mid-fourth century B.C.E., Xenophon (an author of Athenian origin, although he ended up living elsewhere) wrote a treatise on ideal estate management, *The Householder* (*Oeconomicus*). In one section, he depicts a man called Ischomachus instructing his own young wife on her duties. She married at the age of fifteen, and Ischomachus speaks approvingly of her having been "under great constraint" until then, so that she would "see, hear, and say as little as possible" (7.5f.). In the dialogue, she begins bewildered about what she can contribute to running the household. All she knows how to do is work with wool, and her mother has told her nothing but that she must be chaste. This account must be exaggerated, as a girl could hardly fail to see her mother at various household duties and to consider what she saw, but the wish for women to know and think nothing independently is attested in other Athenian authors. Euripides' Hippolytus says in a rage that an imbecile wife might be good for nothing, but that a clever woman is intolerable (*Hippolytus* 638ff.). The logic was that what women would come up with on their own would be bad, so that it was better for a husband to fill up an empty vessel.

Even full of a man's will, the vessel purportedly could not keep itself safe. Men avoided even speaking of their mothers, wives, and daughters in public. Until she died, a woman was usually identified, when she had to be, as "the wife of such and such a man." That *Lysistrata* contains a relative orgy of women's names shows that its world is upside-down and that its women are living the free public life that men did. (*Assembly Women,* a similar farce of Aristophanes, also contains several women's names. But when the playwright wants to depict normal—or as normal as anything gets in Aristophanes—home life, he does not name the women.) A woman had to stay indoors, in the part of the house set aside for her and the small children, so that she would not mix with anyone her husband brought home. She was not supposed to look out a window. Although women were responsible for keeping the storeroom and distributing supplies from it, men did the marketing.

Certain religious rituals took women out of their homes, but the family and the gossipy public would deter them from any interaction with strange men. Some rituals, like the Thesmophoria, were strictly for women. Women could visit each other—but only discreetly and indoors. On the way, as always in public, they would be wearing veils.

Poverty meant some release from control. A household might not be able to afford slaves to fetch water and go on other necessary errands. A wife might have to run or help out in a small business like selling vegetables in a market or training religious initiates. But the poverty that forced a woman out of her home was thought shameful, as the orators and comic poets attest. The son of such a woman, no matter how much success and fame he achieved, would likely never be entirely free of insults. The elderly

and widows, who no longer carried the burden of ensuring inheritance through legitimate children, had more options in their daily
lives. (The older women are the bawdiest and most violent of the
Lysistrata conspirators.) But young wifehood in a prosperous family remained the ideal (at least according to male authors), and it
was a well of dim rooms and monotonous labor designed to
assure men that women were not up to anything.

The legal system was friendly toward the idea of female emp-
tiness. Women could not act on their own except in a couple of
instances that probably seldom came up (oath-taking and one
form of divorce). In the household-destroying case of adultery,
the law made no distinction between a woman who was raped
and one who consented. If her husband chose to pursue the matter in court (and if he didn't, someone else might), he would have
to divorce her (because the legitimacy of her children would be in
question), but she received no other formal punishment; she
might even have had the use of her dowry for financial support.
The men fought out the rights and wrongs between themselves.
In Lysias' speech *On the Murder of Eratosthenes*, a man defends
himself for killing another man whom he claims he caught with
his wife. (The law apparently allowed such killings.) Although he
vituperates against the dead man, he has nothing to say against
the wife who, by his own account, connived in the adultery;
instead, he names her and the children together as victims (4). To
give women the benefit of the doubt, to treat them as fairly as
possible—as legal procedure sought to do—meant asserting that
they had no will and made no choices.

The passivity forced on women created extra burdens. Women
could contribute little to the economy, with sheltered wives like
Ischomachus' not allowed to engage in any kind of business and
having no craft skills but spinning and weaving, by which they
supplied garments for their own families and slaves. The threat
of poverty on the harsh Attic landscape no doubt made the situation frustrating for men as well as women.

In general, the Greeks were warlike, often fighting for each
other's goods, and part of the denigration of women had to do
with their inferior physical strength that excluded them from this
key enterprise. But the exclusion of women from farming was,
curiously, *not* a given. Women, trapped indoors, produced no raw
commodities. Since they could do no work at all unless the mate-
rials were brought to them, they passed as consumers, eating,

drinking—and having children who would cost even more. The sons needed to be educated, outfitted for the army, and left an inheritance that would allow them to get started in life. The daughters would require dowries and were therefore often exposed as newborns. A wife was an expensive and troublesome necessity—a necessity because the Greeks did not usually take an unmarried man seriously.

In these ways, material need clashed with fixed ideas about what women were good for, and the illogical hatred of women resulting may have endured partly because it was itself adaptive for poverty. Estrangement of the sexes can be a population-control device. But to leave such speculation aside, this much is indisputable: Greek men resented women's drag on their finances, and this is related to misogynist insults.

The poet Hesiod (late eighth or early seventh century B.C.E.) recalls how his father moved from Cyme (in Asia Minor) to Ascra (in Boeotia), which by Hesiod's own account was a dump (*Works and Days* 635ff.). He gives us insight into the struggles of farmers in a tough climate and under corrupt governments. Some of his many warnings are against women—they may flirt, for example, but they're just after food (373ff.). In his cosmology, Pandora, the first woman, is the source of all the evils on earth (54ff.).

Semonides (late seventh century B.C.E.) from the island of Amorgos wrote a shocking poem against women (Fragment 7), comparing them to various creatures. He sounds like a hard-up person who does not like pets but has had a menagerie foisted on him. The woman resembling a useless horse is pretty, he admits, but horses are for the rich. The "fox" is a liar, the "dog" a loud, shameless busybody, and the "monkey" a hideous troublemaker. The "pig" sits in her own filth gaining weight. The voracious, promiscuous "donkey" will not work without constant beating. The "weasel" is sex-mad and a thief as well, not even leaving sacred offerings of food alone. One characterization of woman is as something lower than an animal, clay. She is an utter moron: "the only work she knows is eating." The "sea" woman is an insane combination of opposite moods. The rare tolerable woman is the discreet, diligent "bee" with her delightful children; Semonides does not say so, but bees were associated with work without consumption, and with reproduction without sex.

Ancient Greek homosexuality was in part a signal of the opinion that women were not fully human and therefore not fit to

mate with—they were like the creatures of Semonides: not even
the highest one is anything a man would want to be intimate
with. Several other Greek authors touch on the fantasy of having
children without having sex—the opposite of the fantasy in our
times. Euripides' Hippolytus rants about not being able to buy
children from a temple and do without women altogether (*Hippolytus* 617ff.). He is punished by the goddess Aphrodite with
death—not for his cruelty in wanting to deprive women of their
one indispensable function and thereby wipe them off the earth,
but for not paying his dues by performing the action the goddess
presides over. He is not wrong, only extreme. He may have been
a recognized type in Athens. Some parents apparently had quite
a time getting the heir into bed with a bride to produce the grand-
children. The requirement was not to make some peace with
women, but to grit one's teeth and conform. As for continuing to
prefer men's company, socially if not sexually, that went without
saying. The Athenians, particularly among the Greeks, were not
so much exploitative of women as dismissive.

Aristophanes' work, almost uniquely, offers counterpoints to
this attitude. In the *Symposium*, Plato depicts the historical Aristophanes as that rare creature, an unadulterated heterosexual.
The text of the comedies seems to corroborate Aristophanes' preference for women. There, desire for women is hearty and cheerful, and homosexuality a nasty joke—in *Lysistrata*, an Athenian
Ambassador dreads having to resort for sex to Cleisthenes, a
notorious effeminate (1091f.). But is it merely part of the play's
general absurdity that the men, who in reality would have had
access to prostitutes (as Cinesias reveals, howling in his agony for
the aid of a brothel-keeper in 957f.), lust after their wives so much
that they change their politics? What about the women's unbear-
able longing for their husbands, with only one or two throwaway
jokes about boyfriends? We rarely hear elsewhere in Greek literature (with the exception of panegyrics of the wedding night) that
married partners are in thrall to each other's bodies. Normally,
men used wives to beget children, and prostitutes for pleasure,
but even this pleasure was tinged with misogyny. Painted vases
show men beating helpless prostitutes as if this were just one
more sexual act. As for women's feelings about sex, at least from
Classical Athens there is no direct evidence. (The poet Sappho, of
the island of Lesbos, wrote during the sixth century.) All of our
sources are male.

* * *

So far, I have kept this discussion broad and included evidence from outside Athens. The whole of Greece, after all, formed a common cultural foundation. But Athens around the height of its power is worth looking at for features of its treatment of women that are not attested in other cities (but a dearth of evidence from other cities at this period has to be kept in mind). In Athens, trends appear both to culminate and to go in unprecedented directions.

No Greek polity seems to have enshrined misogyny to quite the extent Athens did in the Classical period; ironically, not because of immediate poverty, but because the Athenians had established what they thought would be an unlimited source of wealth, their empire. To restrict the benefits to a small group, they singled out family descent to certify citizenship. In 451/450 B.C.E., they passed a law (sponsored by Pericles) stating that only legitimate children of two Athenian citizens could be citizens themselves. In a way, this was favorable to Athenian women. They no longer had to compete with the daughters of resident aliens to marry the men a recent military disaster in Egypt had made scarcer. But the law, rewarding successful prosecution for citizenship fraud, brought family life under tragic scrutiny. After the passage of the bill, around five thousand people claiming to be Athenians were convicted and sold into slavery.

Much terrifying ambiguity detrimental to women must have surrounded the law. Whereas Athenian men were registered in demes (the local basis of representation in the Council of Five Hundred) and phratries ("brotherhoods," or associations that worshiped a common ancestor), women were not, so their citizenship would have been harder to prove. And how could you prove or disprove the legitimacy of a child born within a marriage? The Romans kept the question in the private realm by allowing only the mother's husband to pronounce on it. The Athenians fought over legitimacy in the courts. Now small social missteps and innuendo could threaten a family with dissolution. Athenian women were trapped, with their own children as hostages to their silence and invisibility. In *Lysistrata*, the Spartan woman Lampito, who is strong and glowing from exercise in the open air (Spartan girls trained seminude or in the nude, like boys), is the object of wistful wonder on the part of the Athenian women (78ff.). Sparta was communistic; citizens had restricted home lives and economic activities and were obliged to treat their children as belonging to the state. Adultery and illegitimacy among Spartans made relatively little difference.

The position of women in Classical Athens is full of ironies. By giving Athenian women a monopoly on the Athenian marriage market, the Periclean law guaranteed that they, who could not walk down the street with their faces uncovered, would share in the wealth of two or three continents. The politicians of the democracy were shrewd in making women into an interest group of this kind. Women, as far as we can tell, showed a strong preference for security over freedom; they could probably not grasp what a worthwhile life outside the home might be. Prostitution threatened, a more dependent condition than wifehood, but with no security whatsoever. (The fame and influence of Aspasia, Pericles' mistress, and a few other courtesans would hardly have tempted women, as there were few exceptions to the trade's general misery. Aspasia herself was lampooned and prosecuted, and it was only because Pericles went all out to protect her that she retained her high if ambiguous status.) The tilting of the Athenian scale toward women's security was therefore radical. In addition to supplying a captive herd of potential husbands, the state dowered girls from poor families, supported orphans and widows, and performed other services women with no earning capacity must have appreciated.

A special problem was posed by the fact that women had no right to own anything yet would sometimes be orphaned without brothers to provide for them. Such a woman would become "with the inheritance"; no one could claim it without marrying her. In the usual case, it would be a paternal uncle (the relative legally next in line) to whom the court gave her along with everything her father had owned. (In contrast, if an unbetrothed Spartan girl was orphaned, the two kings chose her husband, and they represented the state's interest in her future household and children; this probably protected her from incest, and certainly from being a mere appendage to an estate.) What may seem to us a brutal transaction was intended humanely. The Athenians would not have considered giving a woman property for her own use, yet without the protection of being "with the inheritance," she could have ended up on the street.

It would be impossible to say whether or not Athenian women were happy, but they were in all likelihood aware of how much worse off they could be. The Women's Chorus Leader (378) and

Lysistrata (463ff.) point out the outrageousness of female citizens being treated as slaves. Athenian women apparently supported, in whatever ways they could, the laws that provided for them at the expense of other women. In the oration *Against Neaera*, full of invective against a courtesan who allegedly lived with an Athenian citizen (a crime in itself) and passed her ex-prostitute daughter off as an Athenian citizen, Demosthenes warns the jury that the women in their families will not look kindly on an acquittal that will weaken their own position. He paints an interesting scene of each juror questioned by his womenfolk in the evening and scolded for a decision they believe will harm them (110ff.).

What about public policy with a less direct link to women's lives? Did Athenian women's opinions count? *Lysistrata* is tantalizing. To what extent does the play represent real women's feelings about the Peloponnesian War? I would not rule out influence on Aristophanes from that direction. Beyond the presumably unisex concern about the waste of money and life, the female characters' angle on recent events is a special one: wives miss their husbands (99ff.), high casualties mean that girls will have fewer chances to marry (593ff.), and mothers are tired of sending their sons—their main claim to nation-building (651)—off to a war the men frivolously exacerbate and prolong (507ff., 588f.).

The protest is remote from modern feminism. Like the male anti-Peloponnesian War protagonist Dicaeopolis in *Acharnians*, the women are skeptical conservatives. They are repeatedly accused by the male chorus of oligarchic conspiracy, and they do in fact embody an upper-class policy friendly to the Spartans and unfriendly to pork-barrel features of the war the radical lower classes supported. But it is not purely a question of class. Aristophanes jokes in *Assembly Women* that women naturally resist change: they boil dye into their wool and hide their boyfriends in the house "just as they always have," so who better to hold the state in trust (214ff.)? In *Lysistrata*, women just want to perform the ordinary duties and enjoy the ordinary pleasures of life, in line with venerable institutions. Rather than resenting their city, the Athenian women are full of praise for its traditions and consider themselves honored to serve it.

To do this now they must flout law, religion, and every notion of public decency—and this is definitely no reflection of real women's attitudes, but merely satirical farce and fantasy. That women have to make peace is less an encomium of women than a

mockery of the men who have failed to do it. That women characters are farther-seeing, more self-restrained, and more willing to
act decisively on behalf of their city than the men are is an
uproarious joke and a pitiless condemnation of their husbands.
The world is turned upside down, as when tiny Homeric animals
fight in the mock-epic *Battle of the Frogs and the Mice.*

I will end by zeroing in on Athenian women's role in public
rituals, which is symbolically important in *Lysistrata* and which
did much to define the identity of real citizen women. The greatest outrage Neaera is said to have helped commit, an outrage citizen women will not hear about tolerantly, was to foist a girl
soiled by prostitution onto the King Archon as a wife. He held an
ancient office that retained important ceremonial functions, and
his wife performed special rites on behalf of the city.

From very early times, Greek women had had exclusive ritual
duties. Women were the ones who prepared a corpse for burial,
for example. Modern eyes might regard the duties as oppressive;
we might concentrate on the women *having* to do certain things.
Greek women, however, probably concentrated on the importance of their tasks. Certain things had to be done—the women
would have seen nothing whimsical or tyrannical in the need to
outfit a corpse for the Underworld; it was just the way the universe was set up. And as in their secular roles, women had tightly
prescribed activities, but they had a monopoly. Lysistrata and her
friends comically remind the audience of this when they pretend
to dispatch the pompous Councilor off to Hades by shoving
funeral objects onto him (599ff.). In their expert judgment, this
man ought to go to hell.

With the growth of the Athenian democracy, women's ritual
performances grew in scope and importance. For centuries,
women had gathered for certain fertility-related rites, some of
them secret and prohibiting the presence of men. *Lysistrata* contains implausible hints of how drunken and bawdy these latter
occasions were. *Women at the Thesmophoria* shows an important
single-sex ritual deteriorating into organized crime. Real women
must have enjoyed getting together away from home. They must
have been pleased when old rituals were strengthened by being
brought more and more into the state sphere.

The loftiest fertility-associated ritual was a very public one,
carrying the sacred basket in the procession at the Panathenaea
festival: a young girl of impeccable background represented the

favored present and the secure future of the whole nation. But to a well-placed and respectable girl, a whole career of observances was possible, like the one the chorus describe in 640ff. They express gratitude for the honors accorded them and in return testify to their devotion to the city. Near the end of the play, in 1275ff., Aristophanes goes, as usual, over the top and makes up his own ad hoc ritual, a dance with married couples in pairs. This unprecedented symbol of civic partnership would have been highly flattering to women. An end to the gender wars means peace in all of the Greek world. Woman and marriage as emblems could even take over the holy public event of drama, in which women were forbidden to be actors.

The civic religion of Athens paraded women as stakeholders. Over the decades, a brilliant set of ceremonial elaborations came to stand for all the practical things the state had done for women, and thereby gave a strong rationale for all citizens' loyalty: if the state included those who were normally so far beyond the public reach, then the state was very powerful and very good indeed. Did real women accept the rationale? Did they think deeply about these things at all? All we know is that, outwardly at least, they accepted their challenging circumstances with considerable grace.

Commentary 4

Greek Comedy

More than a century before *Lysistrata*, the tyrant Pisistratus, in his rivalry with the aristocratic clans that deposed him twice, courted the lower classes with the worship of the wine god Dionysus, which was relatively classless. The festival of the Lenaea already celebrated the god every winter, at a sanctuary at the foot of the Acropolis. Pisistratus built a new temple of Dionysus nearby and began a new holiday, the City or Great Dionysia. It took place every spring, when no danger of storms kept overseas Greeks away. Pisistratus also made the City Dionysia worth traveling to, with grandiose ceremonies and spectacles.

The Lenaea and the City Dionysia ended up with the West's first full-fledged drama. From long before, gods, especially Dionysus, had been worshiped with choral narrative. It turned out to be momentous that chorus members now took on the roles of different characters in the story. Their songs became speeches, they acquired special costumes, and their action found wider scope than dancing. "Drama" was the word for "doing" the story. Drama divided itself into tragedy ("goat song," perhaps named from goats as prizes, symbols, or sacrifices); comedy ("revel song," named from reveling processions in the streets); and satyr plays, dramas with satyrs as characters.

There is fairly good evidence that during the Peloponnesian War, three tragedians contributed four plays each, three tragedies and one satyr play, and three comedians one comedy each to the City Dionysia. The Lenaea saw four tragedies, two per tragedian, and three comedies, one per comedian. Scholarly consensus has it that *Lysistrata* was put on at the Lenaea. This whole array of drama was subjected to a regimen of prizes. Whether *Lysistrata* came first, second, or third in the comedy category is not recorded.

Dramatic production was one of the liturgies (special services) demanded of the wealthy, a tax and a draft at the same time, showing that the poorer citizens were now in the saddle. When a rich man was chosen to outfit a warship, he not only paid for the equipage but also was responsible for the training of the crew and for repairs during his term. (Just in case he didn't take his duties seriously, he had to sail along on the ship's missions.) When he was chosen as a drama sponsor, he commissioned a playwright (who would commonly act as producer–director), had the actors and chorus outfitted (they were paid by the state), and sometimes hired extra actors, singers, dancers, or musicians.

Sponsors often spent a lot more than they strictly had to. They liked to boast about lavish productions and first prizes. The political capital that could be gained motivated certain rich men to volunteer repeatedly for this civic burden, with all the stress it entailed. The whole body of male citizens attended (how many women, we do not know). The jury was protected from bribery by a complicated selection and voting process. And sponsors would have hesitated anyway to try to thwart the will, with which the jury must usually have been in tune, of the keen and experienced audience. The contest between the deceased tragedians Euripides and Aeschylus in the Underworld in Aristophanes' *Frogs* is heralded by excited promotional patter and images of wrestling and chariot racing. The author of this farce would have looked like a pretentious fool unless drama actually did rival sports in the audience's hearts.

Fewer comedies than tragedies survive, and much less data about their reception. Readers may wonder how Aristophanes, in plays that followed dignified tragedies, got away with what he did. Some of his bawdiness is extreme. And not only could he make the most outrageous jibes at public figures, impugning their sexuality, their honesty, and the social standing of their closest relatives, but the public figures were also right there, a few yards from their tormentors. In *Lysistrata*, the effeminate Cleisthenes is a suspected conspirator with the anally amorous Spartans (620ff.) and the last hope for sexually frustrated men (1091f.). Sometimes Aristophanes blasts the whole audience, as when in *Frogs* he calls them patricides and oath-breakers (274ff.). In *Acharnians* and *Lysistrata*, he sends up a precious patriotic notion, that the city's heroic roles in past wars confer collective, permanent moral superiority: both plays have choruses of proud veterans who turn out to be jingoistic bullies. Old Comedy was like *Saturday Night Live* but was part of a religious festival, endorsed by the government and paid for with tax money.

One reason Aristophanes got away with so much is related to these very circumstances: he emphasizes the public good. The heart of most of his extant comedies consists of political speeches, in which, whether this fits well into the plot and action or not, the actors and chorus comment on public affairs, sometimes in the first person of the author. Here, if nowhere else, stands the hard limit to Aristophanes' cynicism. He consistently presents the parodic free-for-alls of his plays as patriotic obligation. The hero rejects the mob, the militarists, and others who act for their own advantage, because they will end up destroying the beneficent city that makes the good life—including drama—possible.

That is a little about the politics. As for the structure and aesthetics of comedy, I could write volumes, but lots of other (much more learned) people have, so there's no need. What doesn't exist is a heartlessly efficient account that still manages to incorporate ancient critical ideas. (I do want to keep as close as possible to Aristophanes' point of view.)

Aside from the dead basics, no one has any idea how comedy—or tragedy—came to have its particular form. But Aristophanes' *Frogs* is a contemporary critical work on tragedy, and Aristotle's *Poetics* are lecture notes from only a few generations after tragedy's greatest flowering. Comedy and tragedy, being closely related, share so many possessions—and conspicuously don't share so many others—that I can characterize comedy by turning the better known genre of tragedy upside down and shaking it. The facts of presentation, however, are necessary before any theoretical statements.

Physically, drama grew awkwardly under the pretext that the show was to entertain the god Dionysus, not the audience. His image continued to be brought into the theater and left there during the plays. His altar was in the middle of the orchestra, or dancing floor. Although it was plainly considered important to gather together many people to witness his ritual, a modern scholar might be excused from asking whether the organizers were particularly ingenious in promoting the delectation of these mortals. It is uncertain where Lenaea productions like *Lysistrata* were performed, but some idea of the challenges of ancient production can be gained from the ruins of the fourth century B.C.E. Theater of Dionysus, the architectural masterpiece used for Dionysia plays. This structure, which could hold about 17,000 people, is marvelously suited for a small halftime show, but most directors nowadays would shrink from putting on an actual play in it. From most of the seats, the masks and small gestures of the actors would have been hard to see, especially since much of the action took place across the dancing floor on or around the stage. There was no lighting (plays were put on in broad daylight), no sound system, no curtain, and probably only the simplest back-drops. It would have been awkward getting large objects on and off, and it is unlikely that many productions bothered with any; almost all props mentioned in dramatic texts are small and easily portable. The sole complexity of the physical theater consisted of entrances, at least three and as many as five: two long ramps at the sides, leading to the orchestra, and one to three doorways in the stage building. The inability to construct interiors compelled all stories to take place outdoors, or with stage machinery to roll out actors to simulate that they were inside. The only other piece of stage machinery was a crane for gods and other flying charac-ters. I do not see any end to the involved arguments about how many speaking actors were allowed per play, but it was not more than five, and all were men; they doubled or tripled or quadru-pled their roles. An actor's individuality and suitability for a par-ticular kind of role mattered much less than it does today; he was primarily a loud mouthpiece for the text.

Too much space and too few objects were allotted to the the-ater, according to modern taste, and too little time as well. The plays happened back-to-back, five (of the three different types) in a single day at the City Dionysia. On the evidence of their other public literature, the ancients had their aural and intellectual fac-ulties firmly linked. Still, the attentiveness demanded by drama seems excessive.

But early drama was beautifully adapted to its environment. It *was* like halftime shows in that a lot of the interest resided in the chorus' dancing in formation; this must have looked great from the steep tiers of seats. In very few instances does a text plausibly indicate that the chorus, having once entered, leaves before the end. The personnel were on hand to make the play like a circus in three rings. Moreover, comedy favored circuslike actions; actors mimed trying to set each other on fire, doused each other, had punching matches (all three in *Lysistrata*), threw objects, pulled sight gags with containers, and so on. They sometimes even scat-tered sweets or nuts over the audience. Stylized masks with large, quite ugly features identified the characters, and these masks bring to mind the modern clown's wide-lipped painted face and bulbous artificial nose. Other parts of comic costumes were oversized and grotesque—the long, floppy, red-tipped phalluses, for example. Reconciliation in *Lysistrata* was probably dressed in a body stocking stuffed to unrealistic proportions. I think of the modern clown's huge shoes and wig, and of the big, garish dress and hair bow of the female clown.

Tragedy was exaggerated in its solemnity. A reader can imagine the dignity of the tragic chorus moving, versus the obscenity of comic dances like the cordax: the stodginess of tragic actors who would have fallen off their massively high-heeled boots in any attempt to move fast, versus the slapstick of their comic counterparts. In tragedy, actors mostly stood and declaimed; in the text, violent actions take place out of sight and are reported. A character introduced into a tragedy may long-windedly hail those onstage—the actor had to plod toward them. Comic characters may cop feels when they get together, like the Athenian women acquainting themselves with Lampito in *Lysistrata* (83ff.). The forced explicitness of action in drama appears to have helped in creating fairly well-defined spheres for the two main genres. At the time of Aristophanes, tragedy had no outright bawdiness, comedy no serious emotional interchanges, two crossovers Shakespeare made easily.

But if tragedy and comedy did quite diverse things, they did them in the same main medium, language. The text superseded actions. With no stage directions per se (or we think there weren't any: the manuscripts that survive have none), characters usually indicate verbally whatever it is they are doing. In fact, all the subtle achievements that could not take place in the other elements of drama were concentrated in one thing: poetry. In *Frogs*, the showdown between two great tragedians concerns style as much as content and is entirely confined to texts. Apparently people viewing a tragedy were not inclined to say, "Oh, a bad script, but that's not the end of the world—the acting/scenery/direction was good." The marvelous poetic qualities of surviving comedy suggest that this genre had not much less reliance on words.

Neither comedy nor tragedy contained any prose. Both were divided between dialogue in lines of repetitive metrical pattern, and songs constructed from elaborately twining meters. Both comic and tragic authors normally invented a different metrical pattern for each pair of song stanzas (the strophe and antistrophe), using a greater variety of meters than modern poets have even heard of. Although there are definite metrical distinctions (two of the more obvious examples are that the repetitious iambic trimeter, the brickwork of both tragic and comic dialogue, is looser in comedy, and that no tragic chorus ever danced to a raunchy cordax meter), the generally similar metrical format of tragedy and comedy kept them closer together in subject matter and tone than anything else did. This is particularly true of those songs—the plainest heritage from choral poetry—containing prayers, mythological allusions, and descriptions of holy places. The most ornate words are for the gods: words that look outward from the drama's story into yet another world. The reverent lyrics at the end of *Lysistrata* could be, except for the Laconian dialect, a patriotic digression in a tragedy. Whereas I rendered lyrics earlier in the play with the metrical monotony and sloppiness of satirical poetry in English, I quailed at attempting English meters for this masterpiece and used free verse—farther away from the original, but doing less violence to it.

In language lies one of the great tragedies of Greek comedy, so to speak. The solemnity of tragedy and its poetry work together in our minds; we more or less take it for granted that tragedy sounds lofty. It is harder to conceive that comedy could be nasty, hilarious, and sublime at the same time. In English poetry, a reader would almost have to go back to Pope's *Rape of the Lock* or Swift's "Lady's Dressing Room" for any kind of similarity.

On this groundwork, I need to move, through genre contrast, toward an idea of what comedy fundamentally *is*. Aristotle says that a tragedy is an action "serious, complete, and of some magnitude," which creates in the audience a catharsis, or cleansing, through pity and fear. Comedy, on the other hand, is funny precisely because it is not distressing; whatever goes wrong does not cause pain—pity or fear to the viewers, Aristotle must mean (*Poetics* 1449af.).

The emotional contrasts with comedy are clear, and the difference in completeness almost as much so. Aristotle lauds self-contained and logically coherent tragic plots. Most surviving tragedies, based on traditional tales as they are, meet this standard, but comedies do not. Aristophanes produces the clatter of making up one thing after another, and whether one thing coheres with any other seems the least of his concerns. The greatest of his plays, like *Lysistrata*, have an aesthetic wholeness, but this has little to do with logic of plot. (As several modern critics have remarked, if the men in their prime are all away at war, how will they even know about a sexual strike?) Fear and pity arise more readily from an outcome that makes sense: fear comes from the expectation of the outcome, pity from the crushing of a character in fate's efficient and relentless machinery. But laughter is more likely after events unlikely, unexpected, or absurd. Aristotle's work on comedy is lost, which is a shame, because it would be wonderful to see a great proponent of severely imposed artistic order driven to conceding that *dis*order can also be at the service of art.

Aristotle opposes the universals of tragedy to the specifics of history (1451af.). He could have mentioned the specifics of comedy as well. Comedy is *reactive*. Tragedy *is about* the universe; it enacts fate. It does this in a detached way, through myth. Old Comedy *responds to* some immediate stimulus—the closer, the better, so that it could not keep its hands off contemporary entities. Comedy staged at the City Dionysia reportedly dated from the early fifth century, tragic contests from the 530s B.C.E. Even in the history of genres, comedy is a follower. From its content in general, it is hard to picture comedy as ever having been a more independent mode, one whose statements were not outdated a few decades after they were issued. And here is another torture for the translator: how do you make the detail meaningful again? My footnotes and commentaries are a try, but I can hardly claim to have solved this persistent problem. Old Comedy likes satirizing tragedy, for example. Mock-tragic lines—too many to annotate—occur throughout *Lysistrata;* but I could not simply translate faithfully, for lack of modern reference points.

Aristotle writes that reversal, recognition, and suffering are the key events in tragic plot; famously, he cites Sophocles' *Oedipus Tyrannus* (1452af.). In comedy, none of these events has any solid quality. The protagonist may experience setbacks but never a permanent change from good to bad fortune. Lysistrata struggles cheerfully to inevitable victory. She, unlike tragic protagonists, makes no important, plot-changing recognitions: she knows the vital truth from the beginning. Of course, she does not suffer enough to excite pity; naughtier comic protagonists than her get some comeuppance, but never on a tragic scale. Comedy, whose scenes are not taken up with the somewhat stereotyped big events of tragedy, such as the recognition of lost relatives, jumps between incidents of considerable variety and oddity.

Some incidents are more common than others—the feast or cele-bration is practically mandatory—but compared to tragedy, com-edy looks very easy for an author to move around in. His characters' enterprise and inventiveness are a reflection of his own. Conventions like the messenger speech, when they occur, could be called wholly optional parodies of tragedy.

What does all of this add up to, generally, as far as story lines are concerned? In a regulation tragedy, according to Aristotle, a person of importance who is neither wholly good nor wholly bad comes to grief through some "mistake" (1453a). A notion of reck-less pride (hubris) leading to disaster informs many of the trage-dies we still have. In a typical comedy, a person of no importance, like Lysistrata, takes on leadership out of nowhere; earthy, brash common sense leads to triumph. The tragic hero sees dissolved what is close to him, a family or a government. The comic hero unites what was chaotic. Lysistrata brings the entire Greek world into permanent peace.

Line by line, what do the generic differences mean? Broad and basic exposition dominates the tragic prologue. Where are we? Whose palace is this? What is the matter? The address to suppli-ants at the beginning of *Oedipus Tyrannus*, while beginning the action, includes all this. In comedy the prologue—if so formal a label is appropriate—is idiosyncratic: isolated gripes, for example, like Lysistrata's annoyance that the Athenian women do not show up on time. The entry of the chorus in tragedy establishes normal-ity; this group of ordinary people in their ordinary role will com-ment on the action sympathetically but seldom get involved in it. The comic chorus represents the arrival of a weird new world: warrior retirees, both men and women, in *Lysistrata;* deified clouds or talking insects in other plays. They are active characters, seldom friendly to the protagonists; in *Lysistrata*, they fight each other. Whatever strange things go on, the chorus makes them stranger.

Speeches in tragedy go toward generalizations, in comedy toward specifics. Arguments in tragedy involve exchange of debating points, many of which could fit other situations; in com-edy, arguments contain well-directed insults and blows. In its lyr-ics, the tragic chorus cannot even consistently attend to matters at hand. It rejoices, panics, and mourns—but prefers to pretend it is somewhere else. It consists of naive, undistinguished people look-ing at events way too big for them; its poems may go off into the abstract, like the thoughts of passengers in a runaway bus. The comic chorus' lyrics are usually right on the nail; the chorus in *Lysistrata*, for example, sing during their entrance about hauling the lighted coals and the water they are hauling at the moment.

The great tragic poets would have agreed with Aristotle's dictum in the *Poetics* (1460a) that authors ought to shut up about themselves. Even when Aeschylus wrote in *The Persians* about an event he himself had lived through, the Battle of Salamis, he did not write from his own point of view but from that of the enemy leader. Aristophanes' plays are ripe with his personal involvement; he even describes recent events in his life and characterizes himself at length.

The impersonality of tragedy can extend to the characters themselves. Aristotle thinks they ought to be universal types (1451b), and I strain to imagine that he had anything to complain about in what he read. Comedy has the quirky individuals. They suggest real people in Athens and at the same time play on our knowledge of the idiosyncrasies of those around us. Nothing in tragedy (except maybe the transvestite scene in Euripides' *Bacchae*, which is comedy sneaking in) arouses a "Yeah, you're not kidding," in the way that the wives' attempted defections or Myrrhine's teasing do in *Lysistrata*. (The knowability of the characters contrasts, sometimes disconcertingly, with the unfamiliar kind of comic detail I mentioned above, the specifics of the culture against which comedy reacts.) Tragedy is knowable in a different way, in that characters represent universal experiences: erotic love, mourning, envy, fear, and so on. Sometimes the content may seem not only knowable but also obvious, as in a famous parody of tragedy by the great classical scholar A. E. Housman:

> [Alcmaeon]. May I then enter, passing through the door?
> [Chorus].   Go, chase into the house a lucky foot.
>   And, O my son, be, on the one hand, good,
>   And do not, on the other hand, be bad;
>   For that is very much the safest plan.

Okay, that is a cheap shot. My excuse is that I am motivated by the universal experience of the longing for justice. Tragedy and comedy are both wonderful, but comedy is only beginning to get the attention it deserves.

Selected Bibliography

Bowie, A. *Aristophanes: Myth, Ritual and Comedy.* Cambridge, 1993.

Bowra, C. *The Greek Experience.* New York, 1957.

Buckley, T., ed. *Aspects of Greek History 750–323 BC: A Source-Based Approach.* London, 1996.

Bury, J., and R. Meigs. *A History of Greece to the Death of Alexander the Great* (4th ed.). New York, 1975.

Campbell, D., ed. *Greek Lyric Poetry: A Selection of Early Greek Lyric, Elegiac and Iambic Poetry.* London, 1967.

Coulon, V., ed., and H. van Daele, trans. *Aristophane, Tome III: Les Oiseaux–Lysistrata* (6th ed.). Paris, 1963.

Dean-Jones, L. *Women's Bodies in Classical Greek Science.* Oxford, 1994.

Diels, H., and W. Kranz. *Die Fragmente der Vorsokratiker* (6th ed., 3 vols.). Zurich and Hildesheim, 1985.

Dover, K. *Greek Homosexuality* (2nd ed.). Cambridge, Mass., 1989.

———. *Aristophanic Comedy.* London, 1972.

———, ed. *Aristophanes: Clouds* (2nd ed.). Oxford, 1970.

Ehrenberg, V. *The Greek State* (2nd ed.). London, 1969.

———. *The People of Aristophanes: A Sociology of Old Attic Comedy.* Oxford, 1943.

Fornara, C., ed. and trans. *Archaic Times to the End of the Peloponnesian War* (2nd ed.). Cambridge, 1983.

Fox, R. *Pagans and Christians.* London, 1986.

Grant, M. *The Rise of the Greeks* (2nd ed.). New York, 1987.

Grube, G. *The Greek and Roman Critics.* London, 1965.

Hall, F., and W. Geldart, eds. *Aristophanis Comeodiae II: Lysistratam, Thesmophoriazusas, Ranas, Ecclesiazusas, Plutum, Fragmenta, Indicem Nominum Continens* (2nd ed.). Oxford, 1907.

Halliwell, S., trans. *Aristophanes: Birds, Lysistrata, Assembly-Women, Wealth.* Oxford, 1998.

Hawley, R., and B. Levick, eds. *Women in Antiquity: New Assessments.* London, 1995.

Henderson, J., trans. *Three Plays by Aristophanes: Staging Women.* New York, 1996.

———, trans. *Aristophanês' Lysistrata.* Newburyport, Mass., 1988.

———, ed. *Aristophanes: Lysistrata.* Oxford, 1987.

Henderson, J. "Lysistrata: The Play and Its Themes," in *Yale Classical Studies, Vol. XXVI, Aristophanes: Essays in Interpretation* (J. Henderson, ed.). Cambridge, 1980, pp. 153–218.

———. *The Maculate Muse: Obscene Language in Attic Comedy.* New Haven, 1976.

Hulton, A. "The Women on the Acropolis: A Note on the Structure of the *Lysistrata.*" *Greece & Rome* 19 (1972): 32–6.

Joshel, S., and S. Murnaghan, eds. *Women and Slaves in Greco-Roman Culture: Differential Equations.* London, 1998.

Just, R. *Women in Athenian Life and Law.* London, 1989.

Keuls, E. *The Reign of the Phallus: Sexual Politics in Ancient Athens.* New York, 1985.

Kitto, H. *The Greeks* (2nd ed.). Harmondsworth, England, 1957.

Lefkowitz, M. *The Lives of the Greek Poets.* London, 1981.

Lefkowitz, M., and M. Fant, eds. *Women's Life in Greece and Rome: A Source Book in Translation* (2nd ed.). Baltimore, 1992.

Long, A., and Sedley, D. *The Hellenistic Philosophers, Vol. 1.* Cambridge, 1987.

Loraux, N. *The Children of Athena: Athenian Ideas about Citizenship and the Division of the Sexes.* Princeton, N.J., 1993.

MacDowell, D. *Aristophanes and Athens.* Oxford, 1995.

McLeish, K. *The Theatre of Aristophanes.* London, 1980.

Meijer, F. *A History of Seafaring in the Classical World.* London, 1986.

Morrison, J., and J. Coates. *The Athenian Trireme: The History and Reconstruction of an Ancient Greek Warship.* Cambridge, 1986.

Ober, J. *The Athenian Revolution: Essays on Ancient Greek Democracy and Political Theory.* Princeton, N.J., 1996.

O'Neil, J. *The Origins and Development of Ancient Greek Democracy.* Lanham, Md., 1995.

Parker, D., trans. *Lysistrata: Aristophanes.* New York, 1970.

Raven, D. *Poetastery and Pastiche: A Miscellany.* Oxford, 1966.

———. *Greek Metre.* London, 1962.

Reckford, K. *Aristophanes' Old-and-New Comedy* (2 vols.). Chapel Hill, N.C., 1987.

Reynolds, L., and N. Wilson. *Scribes and Scholars* (2nd ed.). Oxford, 1974.

Rich, J., and G. Shipley, eds. *War and Society in the Greek World.* London, 1993.

Russo, C. *Aristophanes: An Author for the Stage.* Translated by K. Wren. London, 1994.

Sage, M. *Warfare in Ancient Greece: A Sourcebook.* London, 1996.

Scodel, R., ed. *Theater and Society in the Classical World.* Ann Arbor, Mich., 1993.

Sealey, R. *Women and Law in Classical Greece.* Chapel Hill, N.C., 1990.

Segal, E. *Oxford Readings in Aristophanes.* Oxford, 1996.

Slavitt, D., and P. Bovie, eds. *Aristophanes 2: Wasps, Lysistrata, Frogs, The Sexual Congress.* Philadelphia, 1999.

Sommerstein, A., ed. and trans. *Lysistrata.* Warminster, 1990.

——, trans. *Aristophanes: The Acharnians, The Clouds, Lysistrata.* Harmondsworth, England, 1973.

Stanford, W., ed. *Aristophanes: Frogs* (2nd ed.). Bristol, 1963.

Taaffe, L. *Aristophanes and Women.* London, 1993.

Tuchman, B. *The March of Folly: From Troy to Vietnam.* New York, 1984.

Turner, H., ed. *Aristophanes' Lysistrata.* Bryn Mawr, 1982.

Vaio, J. "The Manipulation of Theme and Action in Aristophanes' *Lysistrata.*" *Greek, Roman and Byzantine Studies* 14 (1973): 369–80.

Vickers, B. *In Defence of Rhetoric.* Oxford, 1988.

Vickers, M., ed. *Pericles on Stage: Political Comedy in Aristophanes's Early Plays.* Austin, Tex., 1997.

Winkler, J., and F. Zeitlin, eds. *Nothing to Do with Dionysos? Athenian Drama in Its Social Context.* Princeton, N.J., 1990.

Witman, C. *Aristophanes and the Comic Hero.* Cambridge, Mass., 1964.

Zanker, P. *The Mask of Socrates: The Image of the Intellectual in Antiquity.* Translated by A. Shapiro. Berkeley, Calif., 1995.

Index to the Commentaries